"WE HAVE GIVEN YOU A REPUBLIC -

IF YOU CAN KEEP IT?"

AN ESSAY ON THE CONSTITUTION

BY
ALLAN K. STONE

DEDICATION

This book would not have made it to the printers and ultimately your book shelf or coffee table without the inspiration and help of David and Corinne Trimble, Cathy and Stan Clardy and Rex Miller - all of whom have had a significant impact on my life as a living historian and even more importantly my studies of our *Constitution*. As presenters of the truth, they and countless other living historians have served as guides to me in my many years of research. It is our desire to present to the general public, the importance of our real history in an effort to properly prepare us for the future. We hope the words on these few pages will inspire you, as a reader and more importantly one of "We, the people".

FORWARD

When Benjamin Franklin left the Constitutional Convention, and spoke those famous words, "We have given you a Republic, if you can keep it," the critical words were "if you can keep it". Franklin knew, as did a majority of those delegates, that keeping it would require vigilance and virtue not only on the part of citizens but especially by their elected representatives. Nothing brings this into focus more than the absence of virtue exercised in the administration of government and the rule of law today.

Here are some insights from the leaders at that time.

We have staked the whole future of American Civilization, not upon the power of government, far from it. We have staked the future... upon the capacity of each and all of us to govern ourselves, to sustain ourselves, according to the Ten Commandments of God.
– James Madison

Can the liberties of a nation be thought secure, when we have removed their only firm basis; a conviction in the minds of the people that these are a gift from God?
– Thomas Jefferson

Our Constitution was made only for a religious and moral people. It is wholly inadequate for the government of any other.
– John Adams

A Bible and a newspaper in every house, a good school in every district, all studied and appreciated as they merit, are the principal supports of virtue, morality, and civil liberty.
– Benjamin Franklin

A general dissolution of principles and manners will more surely overthrow the liberty of America than the whole force of the common enemy. While the people are virtuous they cannot be subdued; but when once they lose their virtue then they will be ready to surrender their liberty to the first external or internal foe.
- Samuel Adams

Necessity is the argument of tyrants, it is the creed of slaves.
– William Pitt

You see, a Republic is a government ruled by law, not by the will of men. Understand, it is the faith and confidence that the rule of law justly applies to all that gives a Republic its unique position among human governments and gives its citizens confidence in the future. There can be no Legislative or Executive Action to interfere with your legal pursuits in-as-much as those are not part of the delegated roles that the Sovereign States assigned to the Federal Government.

Respect for and obedience to the law has always been a prerequisite for a successful and prosperous society. H.G. Wells (1866-1946) a prolific writer and Biblical skeptic said in his 1324-page tome *The Outline of History* concerning the collapse of the Roman Empire, "The essence of its failure was that it could not sustain unity. In its early stages its citizens, both patrician and plebian, had a certain tradition of justice and good faith, and of loyalty of all citizens to the law, and of the goodness of the law for all citizens; it clung to this idea of the importance of the law and law-abidingness nearly into the first century B.C." He goes on to describe how circumstances swamped and weakened this tradition so that "Every man tended more and more to do what was right in his own eyes." Thus, Roman unity collapsed and Rome passed into the pages of history.

Our Founders, representing every Colony which were later recognized as Sovereign States, knew the nature of their fellow colonists reasonably well and presumed that their efforts, documents, and subsequent agreements and laws would be administered by like-minded individuals; Christian men of virtue. Understanding that liberties greatest burden is the freedom to choose between good and evil they agreed that they would do good and adhere to the rule of law, thus a Republic. This experiment lasted nearly 80 years until the gutter philosophies of Europe infected segments of the population that resulted in men pursuing their base appetites of pride, greed, lust, ambition, pleasure and force. This ultimately meant that they would do which seemed right in their own eyes, regardless of the law. The French economist Frederic Bastiat (1801-1850) stated it simply, "When plunder becomes a way of life for a group of men in a society, over the course of time they create for themselves a legal system that authorizes it and a moral code that glorifies it." He also postulated, "When law and morality contradict each other, the citizen has the cruel alternative of either losing his moral sense or losing his respect for the law." Welcome to the Twenty First Century!

Al Stone has done a wonderful and useful service by giving us all the pertinent documents contained within this small volume along with their intended definitions. They surely demonstrate how very far we have wandered as a people. Observe, in these documents, the use of the term natural rights. That term refers to God-given rights that all men possess as a result of having been made in God's image. No institution on earth possesses the authority to take them, though many have tried. Our adversaries seek the obliteration of God and the Republic along with any history which references either. This book can be an anchor in discussions and debates so read it carefully and often.

Thank you, Al, for this timely work.

Rex Miller
Timberville, VA , AD 2018

INTRODUCTION

It has been my great pleasure and high honor to work with Al Stone over the past dozen or so years in the endeavor of "living history." Al is not only a nonpareil portrayer of Robert E. Lee – many believe he actually "channels" Lee – but he is probably the best constitutional scholar I have ever met. I am an attorney, took two semesters of euphemistically-entitled "Con Law" in school, and have litigated a handful of cases with Constitutional issues, but I still put Al in his well-deserved place as an exemplary Constitutional scholar.

This book is a product of that scholarship. Many talking heads in the 21st century argue about whether the United States of today is loyal to, or has inextricably damaged the legacy of the Founding Fathers and the *U.S. Constitution*. Al Stone understands that without knowing the story of the *Constitution*, and its journey through time with the United States, one simply cannot understand what has happened, and why so many people today believe, but still do not truly understand, that we have strayed far from our original plan and purpose as a Federal Republic.

The way most of us have been taught U.S. History and Civics in school leads us to believe that once the Revolution from England was concluded, the United States simply leapt onto the world stage as a new creation rendered from whole cloth. The struggles of our collective origin story are lost in the mists of time, and in our sound-byte mentality that desires knowledge in 140 characters or less. Not only is this a false premise, it renders one who holds that view incapable of understanding the how's and why's of the formation of our country and the extent to which we have strayed from those noble principles.

Many of these debates take the form of arguing whether we should follow "original intent," or, on the other hand, whether the *Constitution* should be a "living document," malleable enough to take on an ever-changing world. "Original intent" maintains that in interpreting a document such as the *Constitution*, a court should determine what the authors were trying to achieve, and to give effect to what they intended to accomplish, the actual text of the legislation, or the factual situation presented, notwithstanding.

"Original intent" presumes that there is a single, unified intent behind a text, which is in most cases, an impossibility. The Philadelphia Convention of 1787 that resulted in the *U.S. Constitution* was composed of over fifty men, who spent an entire summer compromising and arguing over provisions that were interpreted very differently the moment the *Constitution*'s text became public. Each delegate presumably sought to represent his constituents, but being human beings one must presume that their personal interests were also at play. In this setting, how could there ever have been a single "original intent"?

Yet, as suggested by Mr. Stone in this book, one can look at the language used, and its meaning to the authors, as well as the overall context, to garner an understanding of the purpose and meaning of the text of the *Constitution*. In this way, the analysis becomes not so much the rigid, unyielding goal of "original intent" in favor of an attempt to derive a sense of the unity of purpose and guiding principles intended for our Federal Republic.

The notion of a "living document," sometimes also called "the living tree doctrine," is a contrasting philosophy under which interpretations can evolve along with the society, to deal with new conditions that were different or did not exist when the *Constitution* was framed. The fallacy of this approach is that it downplays, if not outright eliminates the benefits of legal precedent, or the existence of standards that may be relied upon as time goes forward and issues are confronted. The end result? A flaccid, useless document, which we had already learned by 1787 with the *Articles of Confederation,* would never work.

A more centrist approach is often called, in a somewhat confusing nomenclature, "originalism." The late Justice Antonin Scalia was a proponent of "originalism." "Originalism and trying to figure out precisely what the ratified document means is the only option, otherwise you're just telling judges to govern," Scalia argued in a 2014 speech. "The *Constitution* is not a living organism," he said. "It's a legal document, and it says what it says and doesn't say what it doesn't say."

But an originalist interpretation still provides for a flexible legal system, according to Justice Scalia in an earlier 2008 speech on the same topic. He backed up his philosophy of interpreting the *Constitution* literally by citing a time during his tenure on the Supreme Court when he voted that American flag-burning was a Constitutional First Amendment right, despite his personal opinion against flag-burning." The living Constitutionalist never has to confront those things," Scalia said.

Not only does Mr. Stone present in this book a realistic, "originalistic" approach to the *Constitution,* he presents the reader with the case for that approach, and demonstrates how the leaders of this country have, in the years since 1787, systematically torn down, skirted and stretched, the guiding principles under which we were formed. He proves the case of what Benjamin Franklin was thinking when he said, "We have given you a Republic – if you can keep it."

David C. Trimble

"WE HAVE GIVEN YOU A REPUBLIC, IF YOU CAN KEEP IT,"

CHAPTER 1

Imagine, if you will, being among a group of citizens standing outside the Old State House (now known as Independence Hall), in Philadelphia, Pennsylvania, on a warm late-summer day, September 17, 1787. Public curiosity was high, in wonderment of what the august body of citizens gathered within were up to. After all, the group included many of the leading statesmen who gathered in the same rooms some eleven years before, and rendered up the Declaration of Independence. It was chaired by the "Great Washington," who only recently had led the war effort that had effected independence and separation of the colonies from England. Adams, Jefferson, and Hancock were absent, working on other tasks, but others of their ilk such as Madison and Rutledge of Virginia and Dr. Benjamin Rush of Philadelphia were there.

Records reflect that a gathering of local residents presented themselves to these men upon their departure from the Hall that day. These men inside had gathered in May 1787, in response to a 1786 call supposedly for the purpose of addressing certain issues that had arisen since the close of the Revolutionary War and subsequent *Treaty of Paris*. The first system of government for the collective colonies, under the *Articles of Confederation of Perpetual Union*, (first proposed in 1776, adopted by the Second Continental Congress in 1778, and only finally unanimously ratified by the original thirteen states by 1781), had been formed under wartime conditions and were proving.

inadequate to deal with issues and conflicts that had arisen under the new-found independence

Most of the disputes that impelled these men to Philadelphia arose from commerce among the several sovereign states. Virginia and Maryland debated control of the Potomac River. Many colonies protested a toll placed by Rhode Island for passage on a road that connected many of the eastern seaboard colonies. And, open rebellion broke out in Massachusetts, eventually known as Shays Rebellion, over seizure of property of rural landowners to secure and pay debts. Few debated that the Articles needed to be changed. Others, including James Madison, actually intended to seek a wholesale revision and creation of a new document for colonial governance.

These stalwarts had labored diligently and secretly for more than four months and were eager to leave the confines of a meeting room and return to their respective homes. The last thing they wanted to do was to become engaged in a lengthy conversation with folks who knew nothing of the task they had assumed – and accomplished. So, when a Mrs. Powell of Philadelphia presented the question, "What have you given us?" the studious individuals turned to the "old man" of the group to answer her question. With a solid expression of satisfaction of a job well done, Dr. Franklin replied, "We have given you a Republic – if you can keep it."

Can you imagine the looks that appeared on the faces of those in the crowd? Most were simple farmers; some were shopkeepers; a few were legal scholars and I suspect there might even have been a few homeless folks, and maybe – just maybe, a couple who tended to spend much of their time tipping the proverbial bottle of distilled, amber liquid in whiling away each day. At any rate, the expression on their faces most likely appeared to be that of a question mark. "A republic?" they may have replied; "What is that?" Those who had been cooped up for four months most likely offered some small comment and quickly set about to return home, leaving an open question afoot on the sidewalks.

But to Benjamin Franklin, the senior statesman of the group, this was a serious question that demanded a serious answer. After all, his contribution to the effort was a formidable one and tended to establish a path that would create this "new experiment" in governing. Franklin knew that it was one thing to commit to paper a government of the form that had been adopted, and quite another to make it work in a way that would preserve and protect the fledgling United States.

The 21st century news commentator Chris Stirewalt recently spoke about a Republic: "Keeping a Republic is damn hard business." To make such a statement, Stirewalt had to be at least somewhat familiar with what our Founders had established, and understand the concerns that had prompted Dr. Franklin's warning. He had to know that our Founders, in accepting such a monumental task, would need to draw on a number of resources; but had Mr. Stirewalt and others actually taken the time to complete an in-depth study of the resources referred to by our Founders – I mean a REAL in-depth study? From statements made by ill-informed historians, it would appear their study of our *Constitution* has focused on the formation of a new government and not necessarily upon the precise meanings of words used in the document that accomplished that task. Most writers addressing that period gloss over the years under the *Articles,* and appear to believe that the United States sprang from whole cloth upon conclusion of the Revolutionary War. They pay little attention to the reasoning and scholarship that gave birth to the *United States Constitution.*

To again quote Benjamin Franklin: "An investment in knowledge pays the best interest." I'd suggest to everyone that a thorough and meaningful study of the founding documents can and should produce a re-energized society for the 21st century and beyond.

CHAPTER 2

Indeed, our Founding Fathers assumed a HUGE task in Philadelphia that hot summer. After being called to order, and selecting the Great Washington to serve as President of the convention, these men set about to make adjustments to the current *"Articles of Confederation of Perpetual Union"* under which the colonies were then operating. In short order it was determined that mere adjustments would not be enough. The majority present determined that a whole new set of governing guidelines would be in order. "But how do we proceed from here?" was the question of the hour.

By 1787, nearly 4 million inhabitants of the 13 newly independent states were governed under the *Articles of Confederation of Perpetual Union*. It was evident to nearly all that the chronically underfunded confederation government, as originally organized, was inadequate for managing the various conflicts that arose among the states, including those mentioned above and dozens of similar problems. The *Articles of Confederation* could only be amended by unanimous vote of the states; thus, any state had effective veto power over any proposed change. The kind of changes being contemplated in Philadelphia that summer were virtually doomed to fail if a simple amendment process was all that would be entertained. In addition, the *Articles* gave the weak federal government no taxing power. It was wholly dependent on the states for its money, and had no power to force delinquent states to pay.

Where would one look for help in figuring out how to solve these problems? These were intelligent, well-educated men, but even they would not and could not make this all up from scratch. In developing the *Constitution* for these United States, our Founders referred to four significant sources: (1) the many various world governments of the past (their favorable points as well as their flaws and failures); (2) the *Bible* (a true history book); (3) *Jus Gentium* (laws common to all people, sometimes referred to as "the Law of Nations"); and lastly, (4) *Johnson's Dictionary*, commonly referred to as the "1773 Dictionary of America." One might ask, "Why the dictionary?" To that I offer this quote:

> The Dictionary has also played its part in the law, especially in the United States. Legislators are much occupied with ascertaining 'first meanings', with trying to secure the literal sense of their predecessors' legislation ... Often it is a matter of historicizing language: to understand a law, you need to understand what its terminology meant to its original architects ... as long as the American *Constitution* remains intact, Johnson's Dictionary will have a role to play in American law.

These four important resources played a pivotal role in the decision making process at the convention.

And lastly, it has been my experience that little or no thought is afforded that particular portion of the *Treaty of Paris* that established the freedom of the 13 former colonies on the North American continent. This treaty set the stage upon which the information gleaned from all the other resources would build our governance. With this *Treaty*, signed by designated representatives of King George III (on his behalf) in September 1783, the colonies gained their independence. What is most notable is the formal wording used. Remember, King George, as ruler of the British Empire, quite literally owned the colonies and all that was in them, including the people – his subjects; therefore, he could do with them as he wished. And of course that was the problem the colonists had been experiencing, and their reasoning for desiring to secede from the Brits. Set forth below for your edification is Article 1 of that *Treaty*. Please note two significant things: that each of the (former) colonies is listed separately and the declaration that they are "to be free sovereign and independent states".

Article 1:

His Britannic Majesty acknowledges the said United States, viz., New Hampshire, Massachusetts Bay, Rhode Island and Providence Plantations, Connecticut, New York, New Jersey, Pennsylvania, Delaware, Maryland, Virginia, North Carolina, South Carolina and Georgia, to be free sovereign and independent states, that he treats with them as such, and for himself, his heirs, and successors, relinquishes all claims to the government, propriety, and territorial rights of the same and every part thereof.

By listing them separately, the King (and now former owner) acknowledged their being separate from each other, and not a single homogenous entity. The *Treaty of Paris* was not between Great Britain and the United States. His further declaration that they are "free, sovereign and independent states" sustains his statement of their individual identity. By this document and the Kings verbiage, he created 13 "free, sovereign and independent states."

So the next logical question is, "What is a state?" Let's see how *Webster's New World College Dictionary* defines the word "state."[1]

> State – (adj.) "the power or authority represented by a body of people politically organized under one government; an independent government within a territory or territories having definite boundaries; any of the territorial and political units that together constitute a federal government, as in the U.S.; the political organization constituting the basis of civil government; the sphere of highest governmental authority and administration. (n.) a country, federation, kingdom, nation, land, territory.

In short, the definition of a state is that of a government, country or nation. So, let's find the definition of a "country".

> Country – the whole land or territory of a nation or state; the land of a person's birth or citizenship.

The definition of a country is that of a nation or state. So, let's go one more step and find the definition of a "nation".

> Nation – the people of a territory united under a single government; country.

In summary, a state is a country, is a nation; or a nation is a state or a country – or a country is a nation or a state. In defining each word, the most recognized dictionary refers to each as one and the same. Thus, the *Treaty of Paris* in September 1783 created 13 "free, sovereign and independent states" or nations or countries on the North

---

[1] Note: hereinafter all definitions will be from the *Webster's New World College Dictionary* and note the definitions are consistent with that of the *1773 Johnson's Dictionary of America*, of which Webster's is a worthy successor.

American continent. None of these 13 entities was obligated to nor owed anything to any of the others. They were each free to function as separate countries, or join together if they saw some advantage in doing so. The *Articles of Confederation* was their first shot at joining together, and it had failed.

CHAPTER 3

As previously mentioned, the representatives gathered in Philadelphia that summer of 1787 referred to a number of sources when considering the establishment of a government for the peoples of the newly freed colonies. Just what were known types of government and how did they function was the question. Let's take a look at the most common forms of government known to man in the 1780's and their respective definitions.

Monarchy - Rule by only one person: a government or state headed by a monarch: called absolute when there is no limitation on the monarch's power, Constitutional, when there are such limitations.[2]

While a few of those in attendance considered a monarchy to be a good option, the others refreshed their memories of why the colonies seceded from the British realm in the first place. They had just gained their freedom from a King and his monarchy; surely we'd not be foolish enough to return to such a form. We were a "free" people now and should never surrender this, and all our rights, to one man again.

---

[2] For example, when England was ruled by sole monarchs, it would have been an absolute monarchy. Once Parliament, an elected representative legislative body, was formed and Ministers chosen, it transitioned into a Constitutional monarchy, which it remains today.

Autocracy - Government in which one person has absolute power; dictatorship; despotism; a country with this kind of government; unlimited power or authority of one person over others.

An autocracy was merely another name for a monarchy except without familial succession, and to think "We, the people" would even consider this type of governance was out of the question.

Theocracy - The rule of a state by God or a god: government by a person or persons claiming to rule with divine authority.

One of the reasons for leaving "the old world" was the forcing of one's religious beliefs on others and certainly this was common, if not definitive with this type of government. They had battled and defeated the greatest army known to man and one of the reasons they had gone to war was to reassure the peoples of "the new world" that they could practice the religion of their choice. Theocracy was not an option.

Democracy - Government in which the people hold the ruling power either directly or through elected representatives, rule by the ruled; country, state, etc. with such government; majority rule; the principle of equality of rights, opportunity and treatment, or the practice of this principle; the common people, especially as the wielders of political power.

Members in attendance at the Constitutional Convention described this form of government as one that functions at the crude and mindless whims of the masses. Dr. Benjamin Rush, a prominent Philadelphia physician in attendance at the convention, described a democracy as a "mobocracy" and provided numerous examples of how this form of government has always been greatly abused by those in power. While rules and laws by which all were to live were put forth under this system, exemptions were typically made to some, which fostered discontent with others. Stories of how the public treasury was abused by those in power were voiced, and this abuse of the public trough created huge debt which ultimately undermined the system and brought about chaos, mob rule, ruin and eventual total collapse. "Heaven forbid we establish a democracy," was the cry of those present.

> Republic - A state or nation in which the supreme power rests in all the citizens entitled to vote and is exercised by representatives elected, directly or indirectly, by them and responsible to them; the form of government of such a state or nation; a specified republican regime or a nation; any group whose members are regarded as having a certain equality or common aims, pursuits, etc.; a state nation with a president as its titular head.

It's simple: This form of government operates under the rule of law which is enacted by representatives of the voters. Everyone from the President to the pauper operates and lives by the same law; there are no exemptions.

Following a thorough discussion of the various types of governments from which to pattern one for the former colonies, now "free, sovereign and independent states" (countries or nations), it was unanimous – "A republic. We shall give the people of these "free, sovereign and independent states" a REPUBLIC!" Dr. Franklin offered this explanation of a Democracy vs. a Republic: "A democracy is two wolves and a small lamb voting on what to have for dinner.

Whereas, freedom under a Constitutional republic is a well-armed lamb contesting the vote."

And then there is the question of how much authority to give this Republic? To this there were two basic choices: should a Federal or National Republic be established? Let us again turn to the dictionary for clarification of the two terms "Federal" and "National."

Federal – a union of states, groups etc. in which each member agrees to subordinate its governmental power to that of the central authority in certain specified common affairs.

I emphasize a most important part of this definition; "in certain specified common affairs." A federal government is given power in "certain specified common affairs." The powers given the central government of these United States under the Federal theory are supposed to be extremely limited and far from broad. In the case of the *Constitution of the United States of America*, these powers are delineated in Article 1, Section 8. Each state (country or nation) has literally thousands of powers, and collectively they have hundreds of thousands of powers. In their infinite wisdom, the representatives from the various sovereign and independent countries gathered in Philadelphia during the summer of 1787, only relinquished 18 specific powers to the central government. One early Constitutional scholar compared the separation of powers between the states and federal government as being that of the sun, or the source of all power and light, i.e., the states, to that of the moon, being only reflective and derivative of that emanating from the sun.

National – of or having to do with a nation as a whole, nationwide in scope, involvement, representation; established maintained or owned by the federal government.

Under a national government, all power is concentrated in one location, any other governments are subordinate to that one central power. The states essentially would become one homogenous body, not a federation of sovereign, independent states.

I frequently use this analogy when discussing nationalism: In the 1930's the leader of a state/nation thought the radio was a wonderful medium to keep the people informed, so he initiated a plan to have a radio in every home that had electricity. Once it was determined that all homes had a radio, this leader, Adolph Hitler, "nationalized" the radio stations and from that point on, controlled all public broadcasting. Nationalism is "to do with a nation as a whole, nationwide in scope ... established maintained or owned by the federal government," as Webster's defines it. Simply put, nationalism is centralized control of all things.

In the case of the *Constitution of the United States of America*, our Founders specified that each state (nation or country) must establish its own republican (operating under the rule of law) form of government before even applying for membership in the Union of States, the intended "Republic of Republics." While the word "republic" is used numerous times throughout the *Constitution*, the word "democracy" is <u>not used once.</u> The intent of our Founders was unquestionably to establish a "Federal Republic" and not a "National Democracy." They intended to – and did – establish a government with limited powers where the bulk of power rested with each of the states – the "free, sovereign and independent" bodies that formed the union. The states (nations or countries) maintained their "sovereign and independent" rights and relinquished only 18 powers, collectively.

CHAPTER 4

Difficulties of travel on colonial roads and waterways delayed the Convention's opening until May 25, 1787, when a quorum of seven states was reached. As a driving force behind the idea to draft a new Constitutional document, it was no surprise that the first delegate to arrive was James Madison of Virginia. Madison brought with him a draft of the *Virginia Plan,* which was to form the backbone of Virginia's proposal for a new Federal government. A coalition soon formed with the Virginia and Pennsylvania delegations, and the *Virginia Plan* became the starting point for the convention's work. As one might have also expected, Madison's personal notes of the convention remain the most comprehensive source of the proceedings.

THE VIRGINIA PLAN

It was agreed that the discussions and votes would be kept secret until the conclusion of the meeting, and a result was ready to be revealed .Despite the sweltering summer heat, the windows of the meeting hall were nailed shut to keep the proceedings a secret from the public. With the pervasive coverage of the media and social media in the 21st century, it is difficult for us to conceive of a gathering of the leading political figures of the time being held so tightly in secret. What might have happened if Madison was "tweeting" out the proceedings, instead of keeping his copious notes?

Madison's plan and its basic framework for a government were not seriously challenged. Few delegates raised serious objections to the planned bicameral (two houses) congress, nor the separate Executive Branch, nor the separate Judicial Branch. English law had typically recognized government as having two separate functions, law-making embodied in the Legislature, and law-executing embodied in the king and his courts. The division of the Legislature from the Executive and Judiciary was a natural and an uncontested point. Further division of the Judiciary into an entity independent of the Executive was consistent with republican principles that carried the day.

The delegates also agreed that the Executive had to be independent of the Legislature. American legislatures had created state governments where the Executive was beholden to the Legislature. This was, by the time of the Convention, commonly seen as being a cause of paralysis and dysfunction in government. The Confederation government itself was the ultimate example of this.

In the English tradition, judges were seen as being agents of the king and his court, who represented him throughout his realm. Madison believed that in the American states, this direct link between state executives and judges was a source of corruption through patronage. Thus, the *Virginia Plan* severed the relationship between the two, creating the "third branch" of the Judiciary. This level of separation was without any direct precedent before this point. Madison did not believe that the Judiciary should be truly independent, but rather more connected to the Legislature rather than the Executive. At the Convention, this point was fairly debated, and a compromise was eventually reached that the President should choose judges and the Senate confirm them.

Many compromises were made to balance respective conflicting interests. The House became apportioned based upon population, which helped the more populous states, but the Senate remained at two for each state. The House was to be elected by popular vote, while the Senators would be chosen by state legislators. This latter decision was made to ameliorate the radical changes in the new system by retaining a vestige from the *Articles*. The Electoral College was decided upon for election of a president, to balance the weight to be given as between the states' voting. The question of whether slaves would count in determining population was uniquely solved for the time being by allowing slave states to count each slave as 3/5 of a person.

By July of 1787, a committee was chosen to make a first draft of a *Constitution* based upon the points that had been decided. The committee, in preparing the draft, prepared some provisions that will bear great relevance to this discussion. The first major change was meant to sharply curtail the essentially unlimited powers of Congress to legislate "in all cases for the general interests of the Union" which provision the Convention only two weeks earlier had agreed to grant to Congress.

Committee members argued that the broad powers implied in the language agreed on by the Convention would have given the national government too much power at the expense of the states. The committee replaced that language with a list of 18 specific "enumerated" powers, many adopted from the *Articles of Confederation*, which would strictly limit Congressional authority to measures such as imposing taxes, making treaties, going to war, and establishing post offices.

Over the course of a series of drafts, the "Necessary and Proper

Clause" was eventually added, giving the Congress the broad power "to make all Laws that shall be necessary and proper for carrying into execution the foregoing powers, and all other powers vested by this *Constitution* in the government of the United States, or in any department or officer thereof." Another revision also placed eight specific limits on the states, such as barring them from independently entering into treaties and from printing their own money, providing a certain degree of balance to the limits on the national government. In addition, the committee modified the language of the Supremacy Clause adopted by the Convention, to ensure that national law would take precedence over inconsistent state laws. These changes set the final balance between the national and state governments that would be entered into the final document.

CHAPTER 5

Having determined the grand "experiment" of a "Federal Republic" to be the intended government for the newly freed people of the former colonies, it was now time for each of these individual nations to consider if they wanted to be a part of it. The representatives from each of the countries who had gathered in Philadelphia were now to return to their respective nations and explain this new concept for governing a vast array of people. To put it bluntly, it was show and tell time. In order to install the new government under the *Constitution of the United States of America*, it would be necessary for ¾ of the 12 states represented to ratify, or vote to agree to the document –a total of 9 states. To accomplish this, each of the independent states were to select individuals who would gather together and discuss the newly proposed central government after which a vote would be taken on whether to enter it or not. Once 9 of the 12 countries had ratified the plan, representatives from each of them would meet again in Philadelphia to dismiss the *Articles of Confederation of Perpetual Union* (in total) and implement the new *Constitution of the United States of America.*[3]

So, before moving on, let's conduct a brief examination of what they would be considering – what the Founders were proposing. The original unamended *Constitution* consists of seven Articles for a total

---

[3] Ironically, what the representatives eventually did was to SECEDE from the Confederation and enter the new Union.

of 4,543 words, including signatures, and is set forth in its entirety in Appendix "A". Please remember that our Founders were referring to the *Johnson's Dictionary* which used old English spelling, thus in many cases the spelling used at that time differed from current day. I urge you, dear readers, to take the time at this point to read the *Constitution* in its entirety. At 4,543 words, it is elegant in its brevity and simplicity for the task at hand.

A brief summary of each *Article of the Constitution* follows.

Article I: describes the make-up of the two Legislative bodies and how they shall function.

Article II: describes the position of the Executive branch and how it shall function.

Article III: describes the Judicial branch and how it shall function.

Article IV: is pertinent to the states and outlines privileges and immunities of citizens along with requirements for the admittance of new states.

Article V: provides details for amending the *Constitution*.

Article VI: is a sort of a "catch-all" establishing laws and treaties and their supremacy; deals with government debts and engagements; forbids religious tests for governmental positions and binds legislators by an oath or affirmation to support the *Constitution*.

Article VII: the ratification clause.

The "ratification period" officially began on September 18, 1787 and ended with the ratification by the ninth state, after which representatives from each nation would meet again in Philadelphia for the official implementation.

So now, let's review the various articles of ratification, or agreement to this new plan, by the "free and independent sovereign states" as they were accomplished. Remember, this new *Constitution* was to be a Federal Republic to which the participating states gave limited powers as delineated under Article 1, Section 8. Concerns of the "free and independent sovereign states" are clearly expressed in the various ratifications. It should be noted that there were to be no conditional or partial ratifications, so any terms or provisions, including the various proposed amendments and bills of rights, stated by the states have to be read as assumed in the process, not any sort of negotiated acceptance.

The State Ordinances of Ratification are included in their entirety as Appendix "B." King George emancipated 13 colonies with the 1783 *Treaty of Paris* but as the reader has no doubt noticed, there were representatives from only 12 of them in attendance at the Philadelphia convention. Rhode Island did not send representatives. The leaders of that country were of the opinion that it would not benefit them financially to be a part of the assembly and its discussions. At one later point, the country of Rhode Island was the only nation remaining under the original *Articles of Confederation of Perpetual Union* and wrote letters to those now under the *Constitution* pleading that they should not be ostracized and that trade with them should not be placed in jeopardy. It wasn't until the new union under the *Constitution* was fully implemented that Rhode Island joined.

While the ratification documents proffered by some of the 13 nations were brief in nature, a number of concerns were expressed by the statesmen who were charged with ratification or rejection of the *Constitution*. In an effort to alleviate these concerns, a series of letters were published that were titled the *Federalist Papers*. Written by John Jay, James Madison and Alexander Hamilton, these papers attempted to describe, in layman's terms, the <u>intent</u> of the proposed *Constitution*. However, it became readily apparent that amendments would be needed in an effort to ease the concerns expressed by so many on behalf of the people being governed. In cases where questions were posed, the intent of a small and controlled central government was adamantly expressed. Some of the other issues outlined in depth related to religious freedoms, freedom of speech and assembly, a right to bear arms, no levy of direct taxes, the right to withdraw from the union when membership resulted in a hardship to a sovereign state, i.e., secession, and of real significance was the issue of perversion of powers given and not given by the states to the general government. An example of this concern by one nation was worded "General Agreement of Undue Administration of the Federal Government."

Having garnered ratification by the necessary number of countries, a gathering of representatives from those states was called and on April 29, 1789. George Washington was administered the Oath of Affirmation of Office as prescribed by Article II, Section 1 of the new *Constitution*. A new form of government was now in place and the old form of governing, under The *Articles of Confederation* of Perpetual Union has been replaced – IN TOTAL. It has been argued by some, and particularly Mr. Lincoln, that the precepts of the *Articles of Confederation* were still in play under the new *Constitution*. To this implication, one has only to look at the vast differences in each document for a thorough clarification. Probably the best explanation of one substitution for another can be found in the Bible: "In that he saith, a new covenant, he hath made the first old. Now that which decayeth and waxeth old is ready to vanish away." Hebrews - Chapter 8, verse 13.

To argue that the rudiments of the *Articles of Confederation* were still in play is an admission of non-acceptance of governance under the *Constitution* and a pure violation of one's Constitutional Oath of Office, which says that the office holder will preserve, protect and defend the *Constitution*. Those subscribing to Lincoln's theory were truly initiating a "house divided" and were in direct violation of their oath of office.

CHAPTER 6

At the time the new government was installed, lengthy deliberations pertinent to the concerns raised during the ratification period were held, and it was determined that a "bill of rights" would be drafted and considered for adoption at the next congressional session. Of the numerous proposals by the states, 12 were transmitted to the various state legislatures on September 25, 1789. Two of these, having to do with congressional representation and congressional pay were not adopted, with the remaining 10 becoming the first ten amendments, known as the *Bill of Rights*, effective December 15, 1791. Considering their significance to our form of governance, I would be remiss if I were not to include this codicil at this time.

Congress began with a clear statement of purpose:

THE Conventions of a number of the States, having at the time of their adopting the *Constitution*, expressed a desire, in order to prevent misconstruction or abuse of its powers, that further declaratory and restrictive clauses should be added: And as extending the ground of public confidence in the Government, will best ensure the beneficent ends of its institution.

The Amendments themselves were:

24

Amendment I

Congress shall make no law respecting an establishment of religion, or prohibiting the free exercise thereof; or abridging the freedom of speech, or of the press; or the right of the people peaceably to assemble, and to petition the Government for a redress of grievances.

Amendment II

A well regulated Militia, being necessary to the security of a free State, the right of the people to keep and bear Arms, shall not be infringed.

Amendment III

No Soldier shall, in time of peace be quartered in any house, without the consent of the Owner, nor in time of war, but in a manner to be prescribed by law.

Amendment IV

The right of the people to be secure in their persons, houses, papers, and effects, against unreasonable searches and seizures, shall not be violated, and no Warrants shall issue, but upon probable cause, supported by Oath or affirmation, and particularly describing the place to be searched, and the persons or things to be seized.

Amendment V

No person shall be held to answer for a capital, or otherwise infamous crime, unless on a presentment or indictment of a Grand Jury, except in cases arising in the land or naval forces, or in the Militia, when in actual service in time of War or public danger; nor shall any person be subject for the same offence to be twice put in jeopardy of life or limb; nor shall be compelled in any criminal case to be a witness against himself, nor be deprived of life, liberty, or property, without due process of law; nor shall private property be taken for public use, without just compensation.

Amendment VI

In all criminal prosecutions, the accused shall enjoy the right to a speedy and public trial, by an impartial jury of the State and district wherein the crime shall have been committed, which district shall have been previously ascertained by law, and to be informed of the nature and cause of the accusation; to be confronted with the witnesses against him; to have compulsory process for obtaining witnesses in his favor, and to have the Assistance of Counsel for his defence.

Amendment VII

In Suits at common law, where the value in controversy shall exceed twenty dollars, the right of trial by jury shall be preserved, and no fact tried by a jury, shall be otherwise re-examined in any Court of the United States, than according to the rules of the common law.

Amendment VIII

Excessive bail shall not be required, nor excessive fines imposed, nor cruel and unusual punishments inflicted.

Amendment IX

The enumeration in the Constitution, of certain rights, shall not be construed to deny or disparage others retained by the people.

Amendment X

The powers not delegated to the United States by the Constitution, nor prohibited by it to the States, are reserved to the States respectively, or to the people.

One would no doubt see several familiar phrases in the Bill of Rights, but others that have come into common usage are not in the actual text. Perhaps the most prominent of these is the so-called "separation of church and state." Religious freedom is set forth in Amendment I, yet, nowhere in that Amendment do we find "separation of church and state." Many other such phrases may be found floating about in American Constitutional jurisprudence.

With a new and improved agreement between the states now in place, Thomas Jefferson said:

On every question of construction, (let us) carry ourselves back to the time when the Constitution was adopted, recollect the spirit manifested in the debates, and instead of trying what

27

meaning may be squeezed out of the text, or invented against it, conform to the probable one in which it was passed.

And Dr. Benjamin Franklin said:

Sir, I agree to this Constitution, with all its Faults, if they are such; because I think a General Government necessary for us, and there is no Form of Government but what may be a Blessing to the People if well administered; and I believe farther that this is likely to be well administered for a Course of Years, and can only end in Despotism as other Forms have done before it, when the People shall become so corrupted as to need Despotic Government, being incapable of any other. I am for doing good to the poor, but I differ in opinion about the means. I think the best way of doing good to the poor is not making them easy in poverty, but leading or driving them out of it.

Through the lips of Alexander Hamilton came:

If angels were to govern men, neither external nor internal controls on government would be necessary. In framing a government which is to be administered by men over men, the great difficulty lies in this: you must first enable the government to control the governed; and in the next place oblige it to control itself.

And from the mind of The Great Washington, these words:

The power under the Constitution will always be in the people. It is entrusted for certain defined purposes, and for a certain limited period, to representatives of their own choosing;

and whenever it is executed contrary to their interest, or not agreeable to their wishes, their servants can, and undoubtedly will, be recalled.

Could it be that Mr. Jefferson, Dr. Franklin, Alexander Hamilton and The Great Washington were concerned about the future of a free people and the Republic under which they were to be governed? Had their studies of past governments given them some insight as to the possible challenges that lay ahead for "We, the people"? And what was it that Chris Stirewalt said? Oh, yes – "Keeping a republic is damn hard business" and of course the comment from Dr. Franklin – "We have given you a Republic – if you can keep it."

CHAPTER 7

Over the decades that followed, a number of infractions occurred; breaches of the public trust, if you will. Unconstitutional actions by the Judicial, Executive and Legislative branches came to be commonplace.

A few examples pertinent to the judiciary might be readily found in the early decisions of the Supreme Court. From 1801 to 1835, Chief Justice John Marshall led the United States Supreme Court in a number of controversial issues. With this court, Mr. Jefferson's comments about carrying "ourselves back to the time when the *Constitution* was adopted...recollect the spirit manifested in the debates, and instead of trying what meaning may be squeezed out of the text, or invented against it, conform to the probable one in which it was passed" were cast aside. Marshall was strongly committed to judicial power and a belief in the supremacy of "national" over state legislatures. His rulings in numerous cases assisted in commencing the disintegration of states' rights. Only a brief time after its passage and ratification, the "spirit of the *Constitution*" began to be crumbled. Set forth below are a few controversial decisions by the Supreme Court to be considered when analyzing that body and its effect on the intent of the *Constitution*.

Marbury v. Madison, 5 U.S. 137 (1803)

The concept of the power of judicial review had existed prior to this case, and was debated in some Constitutional ratification conventions. Would the Article III Courts have the power to declare statutes passed by legislatures unconstitutional?

Nothing in Article III explicitly sets forth this power:

> The Judicial Power shall extend to all Cases, in Law and Equity, arising under this *Constitution*, the Laws of the United States, and Treaties made, or which shall be made, under their Authority; to all Cases affecting Ambassadors, other public Ministers and Consuls; to all Cases of admiralty and maritime Jurisdiction; to Controversies to which the United States shall be a Party; to Controversies between two or more States; between a State and Citizens of another State, between Citizens of different States, between Citizens of the same State claiming Lands under Grants of different States, and between a State, or the Citizens thereof, and foreign States, Citizens or Subjects.

U.S. Constitution, Article III, Section 2, Clause 1.

William Marbury was supposed to be appointed a Justice of the Peace, but Secretary of State James Madison refused to issue the papers. Marbury sought a writ of mandamus, or an Order of the Supreme Court directing Madison to issue the documents. The Supreme Court said Marbury was right, but that it could not issue the Order because its jurisdiction to issue writs of mandamus under the Judiciary Act of 1789 was an unconstitutional effort to expand the Court's jurisdiction beyond Article III of the Constitution.

This conflict raised the important question of what happens when an Act of Congress conflicts with the *Constitution*. At issue was the Judiciary Act of 1789, in which Congress purported to expand Federal Court jurisdiction to include writs of mandamus. Marshall answered that Acts of Congress that conflict with the *Constitution* are not law and the Courts are bound instead to follow the *Constitution*, affirming the principle of judicial review. In support of this position Marshall looked to the nature of the written *Constitution*. There would be no point of having a written *Constitution* if the courts could just ignore it. Marshall wrote:

> To what purpose are powers limited, and to what purpose is that limitation committed to writing, if these limits may, at any time, be passed by those intended to be restrained?

> This is of the very essence of judicial duty. If, then, the Courts are to regard the Constitution, and the Constitution is superior to any ordinary act of the Legislature, the Constitution, and not such ordinary act, must govern the case to which they both apply. Those, then, who controvert the principle that the Constitution is to be considered in court as a paramount law are reduced to the necessity of maintaining that courts must close their eyes on the Constitution, and see only the law [e.g., the statute or treaty]. This doctrine would subvert the very foundation of all written constitutions.

So, the Court established judicial review, arguably a power beyond Article III, to declare a law creating a judicial power beyond Article III, to be unconstitutional.

McCulloch v. Maryland, 17 U.S. 316 (1819)

The state of Maryland had attempted to impede operation of a branch of the Second National Bank of the United States by imposing a tax on all notes of banks not chartered in Maryland.

The court invoked the "Necessary and Proper Clause" of the *Constitution*, which allowed the Federal government to pass laws not expressly provided for in the *Constitution*'s list of express powers, provided those laws are in useful furtherance of the express powers of Congress under the *Constitution*. This case established two important principles in Constitutional law. First, the *Constitution* grants to Congress implied powers for implementing the *Constitution*'s express powers, in order to create a functional national government. Second, state action may not impede valid Constitutional exercises of power by the Federal government.

Chief Justice Marshall refuted the argument that states retain ultimate sovereignty because they ratified the *Constitution*. "The powers of the general government, it has been said, are delegated by the states, who alone are truly sovereign; and must be exercised in subordination to the states, who alone possess supreme dominion." Marshall contended that it was the people who ratified the *Constitution* and thus the people are sovereign, not the states.

Marshall admitted that the *Constitution* does not enumerate a power to create a central bank but said that this is not dispositive as to Congress's power to establish such an institution. Marshall supported the Court's opinion textually by invoking the "Necessary and Proper Clause," which permits Congress to seek an objective that is within its enumerated powers so long as it is rationally related to the objective

33

and not forbidden by the *Constitution*. Many of the enumerated powers of Congress under the *Constitution* would be useless if only those laws deemed essential to a power's execution could be passed. Marshall also noted that the "Necessary and Proper Clause" is listed within the powers of Congress, not the limitations.

The Court held that for these reasons, the word "necessary" in the "Necessary and Proper Clause" (later also known as the "elastic clause") does not refer to the only way of doing something, but rather applies to various procedures for implementing all Constitutionally established powers. "Let the end be legitimate, let it be within the scope of the Constitution, and all means which are appropriate, which are plainly adapted to that end, which are not prohibited, but consist with the letter and spirit of the constitution, are constitutional."

Gibbons v. Ogden, 22 U.S. 1 (1824)

Both New York state and the Federal government tried to pass laws to regulate river navigation. Congress clearly had the right under the *Constitution* to regulate interstate commerce. The sole source of Congress's power to promulgate the law at issue was the Commerce Clause. Accordingly, the Court had to answer whether the law regulated "commerce" that was "among the several states." With respect to "commerce," the Court held that commerce is more than mere traffic—that it is the trade of commodities. This broader definition includes navigation, the Court reasoned. The Court interpreted "among" as "intermingled with."

If, as has always been understood, the sovereignty of Congress, though limited to specified objects, is plenary as to those objects, the power over commerce with foreign nations and among the several states is vested in Congress as absolutely as it would be in a single government, having in its constitution the same restrictions on the exercise of the power as are found in the Constitution of the United States.

A few examples pertinent to the Executive branch might be:

The George Washington Presidency: In 1791, with little regard for Article 1, Section 8 of the *Constitution*, George Washington imposed a tax on the sale of whiskey being produced and sold by people of western Pennsylvania. With a full rebellion resulting in the need to call out the Army, the tax was eventually repealed.

The Andrew Jackson Presidency: As president, Jackson believed that his authority to deem what was constitutional equaled the Supreme Court's. The "Tariff of Abominations" was a protective tariff passed by the Congress of the United States on May 19, 1828, designed to protect industry in the northern United States. Enacted during the presidency of John Quincy Adams, it was labeled the "Tariff of Abominations" by its southern detractors because it set a 38% tax on 92% of all imported goods. The South was harmed directly by having to pay higher prices on goods the region did not produce, and indirectly because reducing the exportation of British goods to the U.S. made it difficult for the British to pay for the cotton they imported from the South. The "Nullification Crisis" arose when South Carolina refused to collect these tariffs, and Jackson threatened to send in Federal troops to enforce the law.

Jackson's handling of the abomination tariffs and the nullification crisis, as well as the ruthlessness with which he dealt with the indigenous people of North America are further testaments to his lack of regard for the rule of law as proffered in the *Constitution* and expressed by our Founders. "I can break, & trample underfoot the *Constitution* of the country, with as much unconcern & careless indifference, as would one of our backwoods hunters, if suddenly placed in Great Britain, break game laws." He continued, "It has been my lot often to be placed in situations of a critical kind..." that "...imposed on me the necessity of Violating, or rather departing from, the *Constitution* of the country; yet at no subsequent period has it produced to me a single pang, believing as I do now, & then did, that without it, security neither to myself or the great cause confided to me, could have been obtained."

The Abraham Lincoln Presidency: Probably the greatest number of deviations from the written and implied intentions of the *Constitution* occurred during Mr. Lincoln's administration; but then, that should have been expected. All one has to do is review his stated positions prior to being elected and his intentions would have been obvious. It has been stated that during a conversation with one of his cabinet members, Lincoln said, "in preserving the union, I have destroyed the Republic." He knew and understood what he had done, but thought it acceptable in preservation of the Union.

His inner thoughts were expressed on February 27, 1860 when he spoke to a large gathering on behalf of the newly formed Republican Party at the Cooper Union in New York City. His goal was to curry favor with the common man while placing this new party on constitutional ground. Lincoln was not yet the party's nominee for the presidency; the convention would take place in May.

As you've already observed from previous pages, the *Constitution* itself, like no other, confers no authority whatever on the Federal government except what the states in convention assembled gave it, specifically written in the listed terms of Article I, Section 8. Yet Lincoln's one great fundamentally false principle, as announced at Cooper Union, was his belief that what is not explicitly written in the *Constitution* belongs to the Federal Government. Loyal party followers, men of eminence with lofty titles and positions, who knew as little of the *Constitution* as they did of the Chinese language, fell in line with Lincoln. Their recognition of Lincoln's theories made them acceptable to the general population.

Lincoln viewed the *Constitution* as a "flawed instrument" and instead of recognizing the various countries of the union as "free and independent sovereign states," he viewed them as subordinates to the Federal Government. Instead of a "union of nations" he thought of these united states as "one nation" and thus he concluded that no state had the right to secede. Even after eleven of the states had formally withdrawn from the union, Lincoln considered them still as members of the Union, "in rebellion." Combine this tainted logic with his stated beliefs that the decisions of the Supreme Court were unconstitutional, and you have a perfect recipe for a dictatorial regime. Remember, decisions rendered by the Supreme Court (the highest court in the land) become the law of the land and when one goes against these decisions, it is a violation of the law, not to mention a violation of the constitutional oath he took upon being installed as President: "…to preserve, protect, and defend the *Constitution*."

Throughout his tenure in office Lincoln proceeded to shred the *Constitution* with his individual mandates and presidential edicts, just a few of which are:

Commencing a war without congressional approval. Article 1, Section 8

Commenced a war between member states of the union without congressional approval, including appropriation of funds to raise an army and navy. Article 1, Section 8; Article 4, Section 4

Suspension of habeas corpus. Article 1, Section 9

Suppress freedom of the press and arrested/jailed over 300 newspaper owners who disagreed with him. Amendment 1

Blockaded the ports of various states. Article 1, Section 9, Section 10; Article 4, Section 4

Instituted a Federal Income Tax. Article 1, Section 8, Section 9

Arrested and imprisoned a majority of the legislators from the state of Maryland because they were thinking about meeting to discuss the possibility of secession. Article 1, Section 1; Amendment 10; Article 4, Section 4

It has been said that Mr. Lincoln violated (betrayed his Presidential Oath) the *Constitution* more than any other president, although that may be in question after the 44th President. For a comprehensive look at Mr. Lincoln's presidency and his total disregard for the *Constitution*, I refer you to "The Real Lincoln" by Mr. Thomas De Lorenzo – it's a real eye opener.

The Woodrow Wilson Presidency: President Wilson quite literally thwarted the *Constitution* at every opportunity, albeit at a time when the world was absorbed in the First World War, and the threat of communism from the rise of the Bolsheviks in Russia loomed so greatly that it was easier to simply decree and act without a pesky *Constitution* or separation of powers to worry about. Under the Wilson administration, re-segregation of the military and federal government jobs was re-instituted. Thousands of Americans who dared speak out about his war and tax policies were imprisoned, as well as citizens who read the *Constitution* aloud in public; all of these acts were in direct violation of the *Constitution* and *Bill of Rights*.

The Franklin D. Roosevelt Presidency: Many similarities to the Wilson administration existed during the F.D.R. administration. Having entered office at the height of the great depression, he was faced with huge challenges, and then came World War II. While the *Constitution* guarantees due process, it was denied Americans of certain groups simply because of their family tree or ethnic origin. In February 1942, F.D.R. issued Executive Order 9066, authorizing the Secretary of War to forcibly arrest and transport American citizens of Japanese, German and Italian ancestry to prison camps in another state, without evidence of treason or due process of any description. Roosevelt believed Americans of these ethnic groups might be tempted by their ancestry to support America's wartime foes. The United States Supreme Court gave its blessing to these measures. In the matter of Korematsu v. United States, the court held that the United States had a need to prevent espionage that was more important than any Americans' interests in avoiding arbitrary imprisonment. Both the 5th and 14th Amendments to the *Constitution* guarantee that no citizen will be deprived of life, liberty or property without due process of law, but those rights were ignored during the Roosevelt Administration.

The Richard Nixon Presidency: Among the many charges against Nixon included making false and misleading statements to Congress on America's bombing of Cambodia; allegedly received kickbacks on his properties in San Clemente and Key Biscayne; complicit in the conspiracy and cover-up of the Watergate break-ins by Nixon operatives into Democratic Headquarters. Impeachment proceedings were underway, but Nixon resigned before that process could remove him from office.

The Barack H. Obama Presidency: "I was a constitutional law professor, which means unlike the current president, I actually respect the *Constitution*" stated Barack Obama while still a U.S. Senator. He recited the same Presidential Oath as his predecessors, swearing to "... preserve, protect and defend the *Constitution* of the United States," but records indicate he, in concert with a Democratic-controlled Congress, might have violated the *Constitution* more times than any of his predecessors. Just a few examples:

Used Executive Action in direct opposition to the existing immigration law, and unilaterally changed the law for at least five million illegal aliens, in violation of Article 1 Section 1, that plainly states that ALL Legislative power is held by Congress; the Executive "shall take Care that the Laws be faithfully executed," Article II Section 3; Article I Section 8.

Complicit in receiving official emails from Secretary of State exclusively via personal email address – a violation of Federal Law; Article II Section 3.

Ignored Congressional Treaty Powers. Article II Section 1, Article II Section 2.

Bypassed Congress to ratify (without authority) the Paris Climate agreement involving several nations; Article II Section 1, Article II Section 2.

Used EPA to "legislate" over States, Congress, and Federal Court; Article II Section 3; Article I Section 8; direct violation of Presidential Oath.

Appointed 24+ Federal agency "czars" without advice and consent of the Senate; Violation of Article II Section 24.

Issued 23 Executive Orders on gun control – infringement of the 2nd Amendment.

Released convicted illegal aliens in direct opposition to law; Article II, Section 3.

Expanded executive action for amnesty to illegal immigrant relatives of DREAM Act beneficiaries; Article 1 Section 1, ALL Legislative power held by Congress.

Authorized Department of Justice to ignore Section 8 of the Voting Rights Act.

Authorized Department of Justice to prevent Arizona and Alabama from enforcing immigration laws; 10th Amendment.

Issued information memorandum telling states that they can waive the work requirement for welfare recipients, thereby altering the 1996 welfare reform law; Article 1 Section 1.

Issued Executive Order 13603 NDRP – Government can seize anything.

DOMA Law – Directed Department of Justice to ignore the *Constitution* and separation of powers and not enforce the law.

Bypassed Congress and gave EPA power to advance Cap & Trade.

Congress did not approve Obama's war in Libya. Article I, Section 8. First illegal war U.S. has engaged in. Impeachable under Article II, Section 4; War Powers Act – Article II Section 3.

Directed signing of U.N. Firearms treaty; Article 2, Section 2; 2nd Amendment.

Under Obama's direction, the Affordable Care Act was altered 24 times ; Article I. Section. 1; Article II, Section 3.

In the case of the ACA mandate, the Supreme Court (SCOTUS) rewrote legislation and made it a tax, because there is no constitutional authority for Congress to force Americans to engage in commerce. SCOTUS has no authority to legislate or lay taxes; Article 1, Sections 1 & 8.

Obama ignored judicial order to fulfill legal obligation regarding Yucca Mountain waste; Article II, Section 3.

Waived Federal provision that prevents U.S. from arming terrorist groups; Article I. Section 1; Impeachable under Article III, Section 3.

As has been the case with many of his predecessors, Barak Obama did not respect nor protect the *Constitution*. (Note: Executive Orders/ Actions by the president were not designed for, nor do they give a president the authority to use as, a means to override or alter legislation or any other constitutional violation. Executive Orders cannot defy Congressional intent.)

And as for the Legislative Branch:

The Alien & Sedition Act of 1798: An early example of legislative corruption. It consisted of four bills which allowed for the government to arrest and or detain any who spoke out or wrote negative articles about the government. In most instances those arrested were found guilty and fined amounts ranging from $100 to several hundred dollars and sentenced to many months in jails. Freedom of the press and freedom of speech were suppressed for approximately 2 ½ years, all in direct contradiction to the First Amendment.

While any number of violations pertinent to the legislative bodies could be set forth, an important note at this point would be that each of the two chambers (Senate and House of Representatives) were delegated certain responsibilities under the *Constitution*. These responsibilities are part of the checks and balances designed to assist in keeping the President in line. When the President violates the *Constitution* and Congress doesn't respond in accordance with its official duties, Congress become as an accomplice. Recognizing this, it would be safe to conclude that both houses of Congress are guilty of neglecting their oath of office in virtually every instance the Chief Executive does.

I suspect all Supreme Court Justices, Presidents and members of Congress have been guilty of constitutional violations at one time or another, and in carrying out their crimes, rationalized their misbehavior by believing it was "right to do wrong to do right"! With that in mind, the small list of perpetrators and their wrongdoings herein mentioned could be greatly expanded; those shown are but an example of how our elected officials have abused our *Constitution* and impeded the objectives of our Founding Fathers!

CHAPTER 8

Since implementation of our "Federal Republic," some 229 years ago, elected and appointed officials have taken liberties with our *Constitution* until we are now but a shell of what our Founders established. Our "Republic" has been gradually transformed into a "National Democracy," from a system of operating under the rule of law to one that functions at the crude and mindless whims of the then-current majority of politicians. For sure, those same elected officials along with members of the media are frequently heard saying that "we, the people, live under the rule of law." But also for sure, they do not understand the phrase, because the "rule of law" as touted by them is far from what our Founding Fathers had intended. We have only to look around and note that a minority, a small percentage (less than 1%) of the population, in the form of wild and unruly mobs, now roam our streets and receive more attention by the elected officials than the majority (95+%) who endeavor to live a peaceful existence in accordance with the "rule of law."

And what has been the role of "We, the people" in this transformation? Jon Roland said it best in a 1974 Campaign speech when he said,

"Political corruption begins with every voter who votes his pocketbook instead of for what's good for the country. There is little difference between the selling of his vote by an elected official and the selling of his vote by a voter, to whatever

candidate promises him some benefit."

Decades of apathy and self-interest voting has led "We, the people" into this tender trap. The example of the frog in the kettle would be appropriate here. You know, the one where the frog is placed in the kettle of cold water and gradually the heat is turned up until the water is hot enough to cook the frog. The actions of "We, the people" have allowed us to become the frog and the actions of our so-called leaders have turned up the heat until we're about to boil.

The main reasons our Founding Fathers opted against a "Democracy" was that elected officials all soon realize they can continue to be reelected by making costly promises to their constituents and in order to make good on their promises, the public trough (treasury) must be plundered. To keep the trough flush with cash, numerous taxes must be imposed. A good example of this is the income tax. With the passage of the 16th Amendment, the Federal government was guaranteed an income thus fostering a spending spree that has never ended. Many commentators believe the true destruction of the constitutional republic came about with passage of an income tax.

It should also be pointed out that income taxes are economically regressive, i.e., damaging to the economy. When the tax burden can no longer be sustained by "We, the people," the elected officials seek loans, mostly in the form of bonds. Before long, the central government is unable to borrow money, which results in the inability to repay the bondholders. With bondholders not being paid and the promises of elected officials to their constituents not being kept, rioters with increased demands may begin roaming the streets; windows may be broken, looting may become common place, people may be injured and worse; general havoc can reign. When authorities attempt to bring order, they themselves may be abused. Benjamin Franklin put it this way: "When the people find that they can vote themselves money, that will herald the end of the republic. Sell not liberty to purchase power."

Today as I write these words, our advertised national debt exceeds 20 Trillion dollars; and when adding the non-funded liabilities, the real debt is no doubt in excess of 75 Trillion dollars: looks like this - $75,000,000,000,000.00. To "We, the people," this is not a real number, but our governmental representatives have made it so.

In January 2007 I was honored to be part of some activities at Stratford Hall, the birthplace of Robert E. Lee, along with several other guests, one of whom was history professor James I. "Bud" Robertson. After he delivered his remarks, Dr. Robertson responded to a few questions, one of which had to deal with democracies and their longevity. His response went something like this: History has proven that democracies normally expire around the age of 250 years because they spend themselves out of existence. In today's United States, elected and appointed officials responsible for leading "We, the people" down this path are recognizing the union's true state of affairs. Rather than putting forth an effort to correct the situation, many are choosing not to run for reelection or flat out resigning. One might say they've seen "the handwriting on the wall" and want to abandon the sinking Federal ship of state before they can be blamed.

On January 20, 2017, as tears streamed down my cheeks, I watched the peaceful transfer of power. I watched as one surrendered the highest office in the land, and probably the most powerful position in all the civilized world, to another – and only in these United States does that take place. I watched as our Democratized Republic exacted one more of its historic changes and wondered if this might be the last time!

The campaign and election of 2016, and subsequent accession of Donald Trump to the office of President of these United States has brought about considerable consternation, and to be honest, this discomfort is being experienced by folks from all political parties as well as those who have never taken the time to cast a ballot. This cycle brought with it constant anxiety; accusations as have never before been levied were commonplace. Rioters took to the street and engaged in physical altercations; damage to property across the union was unparalleled and reputations were sullied almost beyond repair. Charges of voter fraud and intimidation rang out across North America. Those seeking a more socialist administration proclaimed collusion on the part of the victor and openly condoned an overthrow of the duly elected President in what could be deemed a "real civil war."

Are real law-abiding folks beginning to respond to the replacement of the "Republican-rule of law" governance, with one governing by the crude and mindless whims of the masses? Allow me to offer an example: Elliott County, Kentucky was formed in 1869 and has voted for the Democrat candidate in every presidential election since its formation, for 144 years. It has been called "most reliably Democratic county in America." Party registrations in Elliott County are 4,580 registered Democrats and 429 registered Republicans. Even in nationwide Republican landslides like 1972 and 1984, when Republicans were winning the Commonwealth of Kentucky overall with more than 60% of the vote, Elliott County voted 65.3% and 73.4% Democratic, respectively. It voted 61% for Obama in 2008. Elliott County was one of 7 counties out of 120 that voted for Jim

Gray (D) against Rand Paul (R) for U.S. Senate in 2015. But, in a very telling result, Elliott County voted for Donald Trump by a vote of 2,000 to 740. That means at least 1,571 Elliott County Democrats voted for Trump, if one assumes that all of the Republicans voted for him, too. Only 2 out of 120 Kentucky counties, Fayette (Lexington) and Jefferson (Louisville) went for Clinton. Even the urban northern Kentucky counties across from Cincinnati did not support Clinton.

I recall my younger days when traveling with children and they'd ask "Are we there yet?" And now I ask myself that same question: "Are we there yet?" Have we, as a people, crossed that threshold of time when "Republic" – turned "Democracy" is ebbing? My studies of past governments combined with my knowledge of our *Constitution* has me guessing. But that's just my assessment. I would urge everyone to take the time to do his or her own study. Put down the channel changer and if you're not going to read real books, then search the laptop and cell for the real facts – it's so easy to do with today's modern tools. It's really up to us, "We, the people."

What was it Chris Stirewalt said? Oh, yes – "Keeping a republic is damn hard business" and of course through the lips of Dr. Franklin passed the words –
"We have given you a Republic – if you can keep it."

APPENDIX A
THE CONSTITUTION OF THE UNITED STATES

CONSTITUTION OF THE UNITED STATES

We the People of the United States, in Order to form a more perfect Union, establish Justice, insure domestic Tranquility, provide for the common defence, promote the general Welfare, and secure the Blessings of Liberty to ourselves and our Posterity, do ordain and establish this Constitution for the United States of America.

Article. I.

Section. 1.

All legislative Powers herein granted shall be vested in a Congress of the United States, which shall consist of a Senate and House of Representatives.

Section. 2.

The House of Representatives shall be composed of Members chosen every second Year by the People of the several States, and the Electors in each State shall have the Qualifications requisite for Electors of the most numerous Branch of the State Legislature.

No Person shall be a Representative who shall not have attained to the Age of twenty five Years, and been seven Years a Citizen of the United States, and who shall not, when elected, be an Inhabitant of that State in which he shall be chosen.

Representatives and direct Taxes shall be apportioned among the several States which may be included within this Union, according to their respective Numbers, which shall be determined by adding to the whole Number of free Persons, including those bound to Service for a Term of Years, and excluding Indians not taxed, three fifths of all other Persons. The actual Enumeration shall be made within three Years after the first Meeting of the Congress of the United States, and within every subsequent Term of ten Years, in such Manner as they shall by Law direct. The Number of Representatives shall not exceed one for every thirty Thousand, but each State shall have at Least one Representative; and until such enumeration shall be made, the State of New Hampshire shall be entitled to chuse three, Massachusetts eight, Rhode-Island and Providence Plantations one, Connecticut five, New-York six, New Jersey four, Pennsylvania eight, Delaware one, Maryland six, Virginia ten, North Carolina five, South Carolina five, and Georgia three.

When vacancies happen in the Representation from any State, the Executive Authority thereof shall issue Writs of Election to fill such Vacancies.

The House of Representatives shall chuse their Speaker and other Officers; and shall have the sole Power of Impeachment.

Section. 3.

The Senate of the United States shall be composed of two Senators from each State, chosen by the Legislature thereof, for six Years; and each Senator shall have one Vote.

Immediately after they shall be assembled in Consequence of the first Election, they shall be divided as equally as may be into three Classes. The Seats of the Senators of the first Class shall be vacated at the Expiration of the second Year, of the second Class at the Expiration of the fourth Year, and of the third Class at the Expiration of the sixth Year, so that one third may be chosen every second Year; and if Vacancies happen by Resignation, or otherwise, during the Recess of the Legislature of any State, the Executive thereof may make temporary Appointments until the next Meeting of the Legislature, which shall then fill such Vacancies.

No Person shall be a Senator who shall not have attained to the Age of thirty Years, and been nine Years a Citizen of the United States, and who shall not, when elected, be an Inhabitant of that State for which he shall be chosen.

The Vice President of the United States shall be President of the Senate, but shall have no Vote, unless they be equally divided.

The Senate shall chose their other Officers, and also a President pro tempore, in the Absence of the Vice President, or when he shall exercise the Office of President of the United States.

The Senate shall have the sole Power to try all Impeachments. When sitting for that Purpose, they shall be on Oath or Affirmation. When the President of the United States is tried, the Chief Justice shall preside: And no Person shall be convicted without the Concurrence of two thirds of the Members present.

Judgment in Cases of Impeachment shall not extend further than to removal from Office, and disqualification to hold and enjoy any Office of honor, Trust or Profit under the United States: but the Party convicted shall nevertheless be liable and subject to Indictment, Trial, Judgment and Punishment, according to Law.

Section. 4.

The Times, Places and Manner of holding Elections for Senators and Representatives, shall be prescribed in each State by the Legislature thereof; but the Congress may at any time by Law make or alter such Regulations, except as to the Places of chusing Senators.

The Congress shall assemble at least once in every Year, and such Meeting shall be on the first Monday in December, unless they shall by Law appoint a different Day.

Section. 5.

Each House shall be the Judge of the Elections, Returns and Qualifications of its own Members, and a Majority of each shall constitute a Quorum to do Business; but a smaller Number may adjourn from day to day, and may be authorized to compel the Attendance of absent Members, in such Manner, and under such Penalties as each House may provide.

Each House may determine the Rules of its Proceedings, punish its Members for disorderly Behaviour, and, with the Concurrence of two thirds, expel a Member.

Each House shall keep a Journal of its Proceedings, and from time to time publish the same, excepting such Parts as may in their Judgment require Secrecy; and the Yeas and Nays of the Members of either House on any question shall, at the Desire of one fifth of those Present, be entered on the Journal.

Neither House, during the Session of Congress, shall, without the Consent of the other, adjourn for more than three days, nor to any other Place than that in which the two Houses shall be sitting.

Section. 6.

The Senators and Representatives shall receive a Compensation for their Services, to be ascertained by Law, and paid out of the Treasury of the United States. They shall in all Cases, except Treason, Felony and Breach of the Peace, be privileged from Arrest during their Attendance at the Session of their respective Houses, and in going to and returning from the same; and for any Speech or Debate in either House, they shall not be questioned in any other Place.

No Senator or Representative shall, during the Time for which he was elected, be appointed to any civil Office under the Authority of the United States, which shall have been created, or the Emoluments whereof shall have been encreased during such time; and no Person holding any Office under the United States, shall be a Member of either House during his Continuance in Office.

Section. 7.

All Bills for raising Revenue shall originate in the House of Representatives; but the Senate may propose or concur with Amendments as on other Bills.

Every Bill which shall have passed the House of Representatives and the Senate, shall, before it become a Law, be presented to the

President of the United States; If he approve he shall sign it, but if not he shall return it, with his Objections to that House in which it shall have originated, who shall enter the Objections at large on their Journal, and proceed to reconsider it. If after such Reconsideration two thirds of that House shall agree to pass the Bill, it shall be sent, together with the Objections, to the other House, by which it shall likewise be reconsidered, and if approved by two thirds of that House, it shall become a Law. But in all such Cases the Votes of both Houses shall be determined by yeas and Nays, and the Names of the Persons voting for and against the Bill shall be entered on the Journal of each House respectively. If any Bill shall not be returned by the President within ten Days (Sundays excepted) after it shall have been presented to him, the Same shall be a Law, in like Manner as if he had signed it, unless the Congress by their Adjournment prevent its Return, in which Case it shall not be a Law.

Every Order, Resolution, or Vote to which the Concurrence of the Senate and House of Representatives may be necessary (except on a question of Adjournment) shall be presented to the President of the United States; and before the Same shall take Effect, shall be approved by him, or being disapproved by him, shall be repassed by two thirds of the Senate and House of Representatives, according to the Rules and Limitations prescribed in the Case of a Bill.

Section. 8.

The Congress shall have Power To lay and collect Taxes, Duties, Imposts and Excises, to pay the Debts and provide for the common Defence and general Welfare of the United States; but all Duties, Imposts and Excises shall be uniform throughout the United States;
To borrow Money on the credit of the United States;

To regulate Commerce with foreign Nations, and among the several States, and with the Indian Tribes;

To establish an uniform Rule of Naturalization, and uniform Laws on the subject of Bankruptcies throughout the United States;

To coin Money, regulate the Value thereof, and of foreign Coin, and fix the Standard of Weights and Measures;

To provide for the Punishment of counterfeiting the Securities and current Coin of the United States;

To establish Post Offices and post Roads;

To promote the Progress of Science and useful Arts, by securing for limited Times to Authors and Inventors the exclusive Right to their respective Writings and Discoveries;

To constitute Tribunals inferior to the supreme Court;

To define and punish Piracies and Felonies committed on the high Seas, and Offences against the Law of Nations;

To declare War, grant Letters of Marque and Reprisal, and make Rules concerning Captures on Land and Water;

To raise and support Armies, but no Appropriation of Money to that Use shall be for a longer Term than two Years;

To provide and maintain a Navy;

To make Rules for the Government and Regulation of the land and naval Forces;

To provide for calling forth the Militia to execute the Laws of the Union, suppress Insurrections and repel Invasions;

To provide for organizing, arming, and disciplining, the Militia, and for governing such Part of them as may be employed in the Service of the United States, reserving to the States respectively, the Appointment of the Officers, and the Authority of training the Militia according to the discipline prescribed by Congress;

To exercise exclusive Legislation in all Cases whatsoever, over such District (not exceeding ten Miles square) as may, by Cession of particular States, and the Acceptance of Congress, become the Seat of the Government of the United States, and to exercise like Authority over all Places purchased by the Consent of the Legislature of the State in which the Same shall be, for the Erection of Forts, Magazines, Arsenals, dock-Yards, and other needful Buildings;—And

To make all Laws which shall be necessary and proper for carrying into Execution the foregoing Powers, and all other Powers vested by this Constitution in the Government of the United States, or in any Department or Officer thereof.

Section. 9.

The Migration or Importation of such Persons as any of the States now existing shall think proper to admit, shall not be prohibited by the Congress prior to the Year one thousand eight hundred and eight, but a Tax or duty may be imposed on such Importation, not exceeding ten dollars for each Person.

The Privilege of the Writ of Habeas Corpus shall not be suspended, unless when in Cases of Rebellion or Invasion the public Safety may require it.

No Bill of Attainder or ex post facto Law shall be passed.

No Capitation, or other direct, Tax shall be laid, unless in Proportion to the Census or enumeration herein before directed to be taken.

No Tax or Duty shall be laid on Articles exported from any State.

No Preference shall be given by any Regulation of Commerce or Revenue to the Ports of one State over those of another: nor shall Vessels bound to, or from, one State, be obliged to enter, clear, or pay Duties in another.

No Money shall be drawn from the Treasury, but in Consequence of Appropriations made by Law; and a regular Statement and Account of the Receipts and Expenditures of all public Money shall be published from time to time.

No Title of Nobility shall be granted by the United States: And no Person holding any Office of Profit or Trust under them, shall, without the Consent of the Congress, accept of any present, Emolument, Office, or Title, of any kind whatever, from any King, Prince, or foreign State.

Section. 10.

No State shall enter into any Treaty, Alliance, or Confederation; grant Letters of Marque and Reprisal; coin Money; emit Bills of Credit; make any Thing but gold and silver Coin a Tender in Payment of Debts; pass any Bill of Attainder, ex post facto Law, or Law impairing the Obligation of Contracts, or grant any Title of Nobility.

No State shall, without the Consent of the Congress, lay any Imposts or Duties on Imports or Exports, except what may be absolutely necessary for executing it's inspection Laws: and the net Produce of all Duties and Imposts, laid by any State on Imports or Exports, shall be for the Use of the Treasury of the United States; and all such Laws shall be subject to the Revision and Controul of the Congress.

No State shall, without the Consent of Congress, lay any Duty of Tonnage, keep Troops, or Ships of War in time of Peace, enter into any Agreement or Compact with another State, or with a foreign Power, or engage in War, unless actually invaded, or in such imminent Danger as will not admit of delay.

Article. II.

Section. 1.

The executive Power shall be vested in a President of the United States of America. He shall hold his Office during the Term of four Years, and, together with the Vice President, chosen for the same Term, be elected, as follows

Each State shall appoint, in such Manner as the Legislature thereof may direct, a Number of Electors, equal to the whole Number of Senators and Representatives to which the State may be entitled in the Congress: but no Senator or Representative, or Person holding an Office of Trust or Profit under the United States, shall be appointed an Elector.

The Electors shall meet in their respective States, and vote by Ballot for two Persons, of whom one at least shall not be an Inhabitant of the same State with themselves. And they shall make a List of all the Persons voted for, and of the Number of Votes for each; which List they shall sign and certify, and transmit sealed to the Seat of the Government of the United States, directed to the President of the Senate. The President of the Senate shall, in the Presence of the Senate and House of Representatives, open all the Certificates, and the Votes shall then be counted. The Person having the greatest Number of Votes shall be the President, if such Number be a Majority of the whole Number of Electors appointed; and if there be more than one who have such Majority, and have an equal Number of Votes, then the House of Representatives shall immediately chuse by Ballot one of them for President; and if no Person have a Majority, then from the five highest on the List the said House shall in like Manner chuse the President. But in chusing the President, the Votes shall be taken by States, the Representation from each State having one Vote; A quorum for this Purpose shall consist of a Member or Members from two thirds of the States, and a Majority of all the States shall be necessary to a Choice. In every Case, after the Choice of the President, the Person having the greatest Number of Votes of the Electors shall be the Vice President. But if there should remain two or more who have equal Votes, the Senate shall chuse from them by Ballot the Vice President.

The Congress may determine the Time of chusing the Electors, and the Day on which they shall give their Votes; which Day shall be the same throughout the United States.

No Person except a natural born Citizen, or a Citizen of the United States, at the time of the Adoption of this Constitution, shall be eligible to the Office of President; neither shall any Person be eligible to that Office who shall not have attained to the Age of thirty five Years, and been fourteen Years a Resident within the United States.

In Case of the Removal of the President from Office, or of his Death, Resignation, or Inability to discharge the Powers and Duties of the said Office, the Same shall devolve on the Vice President, and the Congress may by Law provide for the Case of Removal, Death, Resignation or Inability, both of the President and Vice President, declaring what Officer shall then act as President, and such Officer shall act accordingly, until the Disability be removed, or a President shall be elected.

The President shall, at stated Times, receive for his Services, a Compensation, which shall neither be encreased nor diminished during the Period for which he shall have been elected, and he shall not receive within that Period any other Emolument from the United States, or any of them.

Before he enter on the Execution of his Office, he shall take the following Oath or Affirmation:—"I do solemnly swear (or affirm) that I will faithfully execute the Office of President of the United States, and will to the best of my Ability, preserve, protect and defend the Constitution of the United States."

Section. 2.

The President shall be Commander in Chief of the Army and Navy of the United States, and of the Militia of the several States, when called into the actual Service of the United States; he may require the Opinion, in writing, of the principal Officer in each of the executive Departments, upon any Subject relating to the Duties of their respective Offices, and he shall have Power to grant Reprieves and Pardons for Offences against the United States, except in Cases of Impeachment.

He shall have Power, by and with the Advice and Consent of the Senate, to make Treaties, provided two thirds of the Senators present concur; and he shall nominate, and by and with the Advice and Consent of the Senate, shall appoint Ambassadors, other public Ministers and Consuls, Judges of the supreme Court, and all other Officers of the United States, whose Appointments are not herein otherwise provided for, and which shall be established by Law: but the Congress may by Law vest the Appointment of such inferior Officers, as they think proper, in the President alone, in the Courts of Law, or in the Heads of Departments.

The President shall have Power to fill up all Vacancies that may happen during the Recess of the Senate, by granting Commissions which shall expire at the End of their next Session.

Section. 3.

He shall from time to time give to the Congress Information of the State of the Union, and recommend to their Consideration such Measures as he shall judge necessary and expedient; he may, on extraordinary Occasions, convene both Houses, or either of them, and in Case of Disagreement between them, with Respect to the Time of Adjournment, he may adjourn them to such Time as he shall think proper; he shall receive Ambassadors and other public Ministers; he shall take Care that the Laws be faithfully executed, and shall

Commission all the Officers of the United States.

Section. 4.

The President, Vice President and all civil Officers of the United States, shall be removed from Office on Impeachment for, and Conviction of, Treason, Bribery, or other high Crimes and Misdemeanors.

Article III.

Section. 1.

The judicial Power of the United States, shall be vested in one supreme Court, and in such inferior Courts as the Congress may from time to time ordain and establish. The Judges, both of the supreme and inferior Courts, shall hold their Offices during good Behaviour, and shall, at stated Times, receive for their Services, a Compensation, which shall not be diminished during their Continuance in Office.

Section. 2.

The judicial Power shall extend to all Cases, in Law and Equity, arising under this Constitution, the Laws of the United States, and Treaties made, or which shall be made, under their Authority;—to all Cases affecting Ambassadors, other public Ministers and Consuls;—to all Cases of admiralty and maritime Jurisdiction;—to Controversies to which the United States shall be a Party;—to Controversies between two or more States;— between a State and Citizens of another State,— between Citizens of different States,—between Citizens of the same State claiming Lands under Grants of different States, and between a State, or the Citizens thereof, and foreign States, Citizens or Subjects.

In all Cases affecting Ambassadors, other public Ministers and Consuls, and those in which a State shall be Party, the supreme Court shall have original Jurisdiction. In all the other Cases before mentioned, the supreme Court shall have appellate Jurisdiction, both as to Law and Fact, with such Exceptions, and under such Regulations as the Congress shall make.

The Trial of all Crimes, except in Cases of Impeachment, shall be by Jury; and such Trial shall be held in the State where the said Crimes shall have been committed; but when not committed within any State, the Trial shall be at such Place or Places as the Congress may by Law have directed.

Section. 3.

Treason against the United States, shall consist only in levying War against them, or in adhering to their Enemies, giving them Aid and Comfort. No Person shall be convicted of Treason unless on the Testimony of two Witnesses to the same overt Act, or on Confession in open Court.

The Congress shall have Power to declare the Punishment of Treason, but no Attainder of Treason shall work Corruption of Blood, or Forfeiture except during the Life of the Person attainted.

Article. IV.

Section. 1.

Full Faith and Credit shall be given in each State to the public Acts, Records, and judicial Proceedings of every other State. And the

Congress may by general Laws prescribe the Manner in which such Acts, Records and Proceedings shall be proved, and the Effect thereof.

Section. 2.

The Citizens of each State shall be entitled to all Privileges and Immunities of Citizens in the several States.

A Person charged in any State with Treason, Felony, or other Crime, who shall flee from Justice, and be found in another State, shall on Demand of the executive Authority of the State from which he fled, be delivered up, to be removed to the State having Jurisdiction of the Crime.

No Person held to Service or Labour in one State, under the Laws thereof, escaping into another, shall, in Consequence of any Law or Regulation therein, be discharged from such Service or Labour, but shall be delivered up on Claim of the Party to whom such Service or Labour may be due.

Section. 3.

New States may be admitted by the Congress into this Union; but no new State shall be formed or erected within the Jurisdiction of any other State; nor any State be formed by the Junction of two or more States, or Parts of States, without the Consent of the Legislatures of the States concerned as well as of the Congress.

The Congress shall have Power to dispose of and make all needful Rules and Regulations respecting the Territory or other Property belonging to the United States; and nothing in this Constitution shall be so construed as to Prejudice any Claims of the United States, or of any particular State.

Section. 4.

The United States shall guarantee to every State in this Union a Republican Form of Government, and shall protect each of them against Invasion; and on Application of the Legislature, or of the Executive (when the Legislature cannot be convened), against domestic Violence.

Article. V.

The Congress, whenever two thirds of both Houses shall deem it necessary, shall propose Amendments to this Constitution, or, on the Application of the Legislatures of two thirds of the several States, shall call a Convention for proposing Amendments, which, in either Case, shall be valid to all Intents and Purposes, as Part of this Constitution, when ratified by the Legislatures of three fourths of the several States, or by Conventions in three fourths thereof, as the one or the other Mode of Ratification may be proposed by the Congress; Provided that no Amendment which may be made prior to the Year One thousand eight hundred and eight shall in any Manner affect the first and fourth Clauses in the Ninth Section of the first Article; and that no State, without its Consent, shall be deprived of its equal Suffrage in the Senate.

Article. VI.

All Debts contracted and Engagements entered into, before the Adoption of this Constitution, shall be as valid against the United States under this Constitution, as under the Confederation.

This Constitution, and the Laws of the United States which shall be made in Pursuance thereof; and all Treaties made, or which shall be made, under the Authority of the United States, shall be the supreme Law of the Land; and the Judges in every State shall be bound thereby, any Thing in the Constitution or Laws of any State to the Contrary notwithstanding.

The Senators and Representatives before mentioned, and the Members of the several State Legislatures, and all executive and judicial Officers, both of the United States and of the several States, shall be bound by Oath or Affirmation, to support this Constitution; but no religious Test shall ever be required as a Qualification to any Office or public Trust under the United States.

Article. VII.

The Ratification of the Conventions of nine States, shall be sufficient for the Establishment of this Constitution between the States so ratifying the Same.

The Word, "the," being interlined between the seventh and eighth Lines of the first Page, The Word "Thirty" being partly written on an Erazure in the fifteenth Line of the first Page, The Words "is tried" being interlined between the thirty second and thirty third Lines of the first Page and the Word "the" being interlined between the forty third and forty fourth Lines of the second Page.

Attest William Jackson Secretary

done in Convention by the Unanimous Consent of the States present the Seventeenth Day of September in the Year of our Lord one thousand seven hundred and Eighty seven and of the Independence of the United States of America the Twelfth In witness whereof We have hereunto subscribed our Names,

G°. Washington

Presidt and deputy from Virginia"

APPENDIX B
ORDINANCES OF RATIFICATION FROM THE COLONIES

APPENDIX B
ORDINANCES OF RATIFICATION FROM THE COLONIES

- Delaware: December 7, 1787 = "We, the deputies of the people of the Delaware state, in Convention met, having taken in our serious consideration the Federal Constitution proposed and agreed upon by the deputies of the United States in a General Convention held at the city of Philadelphia, on the seventeenth day of September, in the year of our Lord one thousand seven hundred and eighty-seven, have approved, assented to, ratified, and confirmed, and by these presents do, in virtue of the power and authority to us given, for and in behalf of ourselves and our constituents, fully, freely, and entirely approve of, assent to, ratify, and confirm, the said Constitution.

Done in Convention, at Dover, this seventh day of December, in the year aforesaid, and in the year of the independence of the United States of America the twelfth."

- Pennsylvania: December 12, 1787 = "In the Name of the People of Pennsylvania.

Be it known unto all men, that we, the delegates of the people of the commonwealth of Pennsylvania, in General Convention assembled, have assented to and ratified, and by these presents do, in the name and by the authority of the same people, and for ourselves, assent to and ratify the foregoing Constitution for the United States of America.

Done in Convention at Philadelphia, the twelfth day of December, in the year of our Lord one thousand seven hundred and eighty-seven, and of the independence of the United States of America the twelfth. In witness whereof, we have hereunto subscribed our names."

- New Jersey: December 18, 1787 = "Whereas a Convention of delegates from the following states, viz., — New Hampshire, Massachusetts, Connecticut, New York, New Jersey, Pennsylvania, Delaware, Maryland, Virginia, North Carolina, South Carolina, and Georgia, — met at Philadelphia, for the purpose of deliberating on, and forming, a Constitution for the United States of America, — finished their session on the 17th day of September last, and reported to Congress the form which they had agreed upon, in the words following, viz.:

(A copy of the Constitution was included in the ratification document.)

And whereas Congress, on the 28th day of September last, unanimously did resolve, "That the said report, with the resolutions and letter accompanying the same, be transmitted to the several legislatures, in order to be submitted to a convention of delegates, chosen in each state by the people thereof, in conformity to the resolves of the Convention made and provided in that case;"

And whereas the legislature of this state did, on the 29th day of October last, resolve in the words following, viz., "Resolved, unanimously, That it be recommended to such of the inhabitants of this state as are entitled to vote for representatives in General Assembly, to meet in their respective counties on the fourth Tuesday in November next, at the several places fixed by law for holding the annual elections, to choose three suitable persons to serve as delegates from each county in a state Convention, for the purposes hereinbefore mentioned, and that the same be conducted agreeably to the mode, and conformably with the rules and regulations, prescribed for conducting such elections; —

"Resolved, unanimously, That the persons so elected to serve in state Convention, do assemble and meet together on the second Tuesday in December next, at Trenton, in the county of Hunterdon, then and there to take into consideration the aforesaid Constitution and if approved of by them, finally to ratify the same, in behalf and on the part of this state, and make report thereof to the United States in Congress assembled, in conformity with the resolutions thereto annexed.

"Resolved, That the sheriffs of the respective counties of this state shall be, and they are hereby, required to give as timely notice as may be, by advertisements, to the people of their counties, of the time, place, and purpose of holding elections, as aforesaid."

And whereas the legislature of this state did also, on the 1st day of November last, make and pass the following act, viz., "An Act to authorize the people of this state to meet in convention, deliberate upon, agree to, and ratify, the Constitution of the United States proposed by the late General Convention, — Be it enacted by the Council and General Assembly of this state, and it is hereby enacted by the authority of the same, that it shall and may be lawful for the people thereof, by their delegates, to meet in Convention to deliberate upon, and, if approved of by them, to ratify, the Constitution for the United States proposed by the General Convention held at Philadelphia, and every act, matter, and clause, therein contained, conformedly to the resolutions of the legislature passed the 29th day of October, 1787, — any law, usage, or custom, to the contrary in any wise notwithstanding;"

Now be it known, that we, the delegates of the state of New Jersey, chosen by the people thereof, for the purpose aforesaid, having maturely deliberated on and considered the aforesaid proposed Constitution, do hereby, for and on the behalf of the people of the said state of New Jersey, agree to, ratify, and confirm, the same and every part thereof. Done in Convention, by the unanimous consent of the members present, this 18th day of December, in the year of our Lord 1787, and of the independence of the United States of America the twelfth.

- Georgia: January 2, 1788 = "In Convention, Wednesday, January 2d, 1788.

To all to whom these Presents shall come, Greeting.

Whereas the form of a Constitution for the government of the United States of America, was, on the 17th day of September, 1787, agreed upon and reported to Congress by the deputies of the said United States convened in Philadelphia, which said Constitution is written in the words following, to wit: —

And whereas the United States in Congress assembled did, on the 28th day of September, 1787, resolve, unanimously, "That the said report, with the resolutions and letter accompanying the same, be transmitted to the several legislatures, in order to be submitted to a Convention of delegates chosen in each state by the people thereof, in conformity to the resolves of the Convention made and provided in that case;" —

And whereas the legislature of the state of Georgia did, on the 26th day of October, 1787, in pursuance of the above-recited resolution of Congress, resolve, That a Convention be elected on the day of the next general election, and in the same manner that representatives are elected; and that the said Convention consist of not more than three members from each county; and that the said Convention should meet at Augusta, on the 4th Tuesday in December then next, and, as soon thereafter as convenient, proceed to consider the said report and resolutions, and to adopt or reject any part or the whole thereof; —

Now know ye, that we, the delegates of the people of the state of Georgia, in Convention met, pursuant to the resolutions of the legislature aforesaid, having taken into our serious consideration the said Constitution, have assented to, ratified, and adopted, and by these presents do, in virtue of the powers and authority to us given by the people of the said state for that purpose, for and in behalf of ourselves and our constituents, fully and entirely assent to, ratify, and adopt, the said Constitution.

Done in Convention, at Augusta, in the said state, on the 2d day of January, in the year of our Lord 1788, and of the independence of the United States the 12th."

- Connecticut: January 9, 1788 = "In the Name of the People of the State of Connecticut.

We, the delegates of the people of said state, in general Convention assembled, pursuant to an act of the legislature in October last, have assented to, and ratified, and by these presents do assent to, on the 17th day of September, A. D. 1787, for the United States of America.

Done in Convention, this 9th day of January, A. D. 1788.

- Massachusetts: February 6, 1788 = "The Convention having impartially discussed, and fully considered, the Constitution for the United States of America, reported to Congress by the Convention of Delegates from the United States of America, and submitted to us by a resolution of the General Court of the said commonwealth, passed the 25th day of October last past, — and acknowledging, with grateful hearts, the goodness of the Supreme Ruler of the universe in affording the people of the United States, in the course of his providence, an opportunity, deliberately and peaceably, without fraud or surprise, of entering into an explicit and solemn compact with each other, by assenting to and ratifying a new Constitution, in order to form a more perfect union, establish justice, insure domestic tranquillity, provide for the common defence, promote the general welfare, and secure the blessings of liberty to themselves and their posterity, — do, in the name and in behalf of the people of the commonwealth of Massachusetts, assent to and ratify the said Constitution for the United States of America.

And as it is the opinion of this Convention, that certain amendments and alterations in the said Constitution would remove the fears, and quiet the apprehensions, of many of the good people of this commonwealth, and more effectually guard against an undue administration of the federal government, — the Convention do therefore recommend that the following alterations and provisions be introduced into the said Constitution: —

I. That it be explicitly declared that all powers not expressly delegated by the aforesaid Constitution are reserved to the several states, to be by them exercised.

II. That there shall be one representative to every thirty thousand persons, according to the census mentioned in the Constitution, until the whole number of the representatives amounts to two hundred.

III. That Congress do not exercise the powers vested in them by the 4th section of the 1st article, but in cases where a state shall neglect or refuse to make the regulations therein mentioned, or shall make regulations subversive of the rights of the people to a free and equal representation in Congress, agreeably to the Constitution.

IV. That Congress do not lay direct taxes but when the moneys arising from the impost and excise are insufficient for the public exigencies, nor then until Congress shall have first made a requisition upon the states to assess, levy, and pay, their respective proportions of such requisition, agreeably to the census fixed in the said Constitution, in such way and manner as the legislatures of the states shall think best; and in such case, if any state shall neglect or refuse to pay its proportion, pursuant to such requisition, then Congress may assess and levy such state's proportion, together with interest thereon at the rate of six per cent. per annum, from the time of payment prescribed in such requisition.

V. That Congress erect no company of merchants with exclusive advantages of commerce.

VI. That no person shall be tried for any crime by which he may incur an infamous punishment, or loss of life, until he be first indicted by a grand jury, except in such cases as may arise in the government and regulation of the land and naval forces.

VII. The Supreme Judicial Federal Court shall have no jurisdiction of causes between citizens of different states, unless the matter in dispute, whether it concerns the realty or personalty, be of the value of three thousand dollars at the least; nor shall the federal judicial powers extend to any actions between citizens of different states, where the matter in dispute, whether it concerns the realty or personalty, is not of the value of fifteen hundred dollars at least.

VIII. In civil actions between citizens of different states, every issue of fact, arising in actions at common law, shall be tried by a jury, if the parties, or either of them, request it.

IX. Congress shall at no time consent that any person, holding an office of trust or profit under the United States, shall accept of a title of nobility, or any other title or office, from any king, prince, or foreign state.

And the Convention do, in the name and in behalf of the people of this commonwealth, enjoin it upon their representatives in Congress, at all times, until the alterations and provisions aforesaid have been considered, agreeably to the 5th article of the said Constitution, to exert all their influence, and use all reasonable and legal methods, to obtain a ratification of the said alterations and provisions, in such manner as is provided in the said article.

And that the United States in Congress assembled may have due notice of the assent and ratification of the said Constitution by this Convention, it is Resolved, That the assent and ratification aforesaid be engrossed on parchment, together with the recommendation and injunction aforesaid, and with this resolution; and that his excellency, John Hancock, Esq., president, and the Hon. William Cushing, Esq., vice-president of this Convention, transmit the same, countersigned by the secretary of the Convention, under their hands and seals, to the United States in Congress assembled.

JOHN HANCOCK, President.

WILLIAM CUSHING, Vice-President.

George Richards Minot, Secretary.

Pursuant to the resolution aforesaid, we, the president and vice-president above named, do hereby transmit to the United States in Congress assembled the same resolution, with the above assent and ratification of the Constitution aforesaid, for the United States, and the recommendation and injunction above specified."

- Maryland: April 28, 1788 = "In Convention of the Delegates of the People of the State of Maryland, April 28, 1788.

We, the delegates of the people of the state of Maryland, having fully considered the Constitution of the United States of America, reported to Congress by the Convention of deputies from the United States of America, held in Philadelphia, on the 17th day of September, in the year 1787, of which the annexed is a copy, and submitted to us by a resolution of the General Assembly of Maryland, in November session, 1787, do, for ourselves, and in the name and on the behalf of the people of this state, assent to and ratify the said Constitution.

In witness whereof, we have hereunto subscribed our names."

- South Carolina: May 23, 1788 = "In Convention of the people of the state of South Carolina, by their representatives, held in the city of Charleston, on Monday the 12th day of May, and continued by divers adjournments to Friday, the 23d day of May, Anno Domini 1788, and in the 12th year of the independence of the United States of America.

The Convention, having maturely considered the Constitution, or form of government, reported to Congress by the Convention of Delegates from the United States of America, and submitted to them by a resolution of the legislature of this state, passed the 17th and 18th days of February last, in order to form a more perfect union, establish justice, insure domestic tranquillity, provide for the common defence, promote the general welfare, and secure the blessings of liberty to the people of the said United States, and their posterity, — Do, in the name and behalf of the people of this state, hereby assent to and ratify the said Constitution.

Done in Convention, the 23d day of May, in the year of our Lord 1788, and of the independence of the United States of America the twelfth.

THOMAS PINCKNEY, President.

Attest. John Sandford Dart, Secretary.

And whereas it is essential to the preservation of the rights reserved to the several states, and the freedom of the people, under the operations of a general government, that the right of prescribing the manner, time, and places, of holding the elections to the federal legislature, should be forever inseparably annexed to the sovereignty of the several states, — This Convention doth declare, that the same ought to remain, to all posterity, a perpetual and fundamental right in the local, exclusive of the interference of the general government, except in cases where the legislatures of the states shall refuse or neglect to perform and fulfil the same, according to the tenor of the said Constitution.

This Convention doth also declare, that no section or paragraph of the said Constitution warrants a construction that the states do not retain every power not expressly relinquished by them, and vested in the general government of the Union.

Resolved, That the general government of the United States ought never to impose direct taxes, but where the moneys arising from the duties, imports, and excise, are insufficient for the public exigencies, nor then until Congress shall have made a requisition upon the states to assess, levy, and pay, their respective proportions of such requisitions; and in case any state shall neglect or refuse to pay its proportion, pursuant to such requisition, then Congress may assess and levy such state's proportion, together with interest thereon, at the rate of six per centum per annum, from the time of payment prescribed by such requisition.

Resolved, That the third section of the sixth article ought to be amended, by inserting the word "other" between the words "no" and "religious."

Resolved, That it be a standing instruction to all such delegates as may hereafter be elected to represent this state in the general government, to exert their utmost abilities and influence to effect an alteration of the Constitution, conformably to the aforegoing resolutions.

Done in Convention, the 23d day of May, in the year of our Lord 1788, and of the independence of the United States of America the twelfth.

THOMAS PINCKNEY, President.

Attest. John Sandford Dart, Secretary."

- New Hampshire: June 21, 1788 (With this state's ratification, the Constitution was sufficient to be officially implemented) = "In Convention of the Delegates of the People of the State of New Hampshire, June the 21st, 1788.

The Convention having impartially discussed and fully considered the Constitution for the United States of America, reported to Congress by the Convention of Delegates from the United States of America, and submitted to us by a resolution of the General Court of said state, passed the 14th day of December last past, and acknowledging with grateful hearts the goodness of the Supreme Ruler of the universe in affording the people of the United States, in the course of his providence, an opportunity, deliberately and peaceably, without fraud of surprise, of entering into an explicit and solemn compact with each other, by assenting to and ratifying a new Constitution, in order to form a more perfect union, establish justice, insure domestic tranquillity, provide for the common defence, promote the general welfare, and secure the blessings of liberty to themselves and their posterity, — Do, in the name and behalf of the people of the state of New Hampshire, assent to and ratify the said Constitution for the United States of America. And as it is the opinion of this Convention, that certain amendments and alterations in the said Constitution would remove the fears and quiet the apprehensions of many of the good people of this state, and more effectually guard against an undue administration of the federal government, — The Convention do therefore recommend that the following alterations and provisions be introduced in the said Constitution: —

I. That it be explicitly declared that all powers not expressly and particularly delegated by the aforesaid Constitution are reserved to the several states, to be by them exercised.

II. That there shall be one representative to every thirty thousand persons, according to the census mentioned in the Constitution, until the whole number of representatives amount to two hundred.

III. That Congress do not exercise the powers vested in them by the fourth section of the first article but in cases when a state shall neglect or refuse to make the regulations therein mentioned, or shall make regulations subversive of the rights of the people to a free and equal representation in Congress; nor shall Congress in any case make regulations contrary to a free and equal representation.

IV. That Congress do not lay direct taxes but when the moneys arising from impost, excise, and their other resources, are insufficient for the public exigencies, nor then, until Congress shall have first made a requisition upon the states to assess, levy, and pay, their respective proportions of such requisition, agreeably to the census fixed in the said Constitution, in such way and manner as the legislature of the state shall think best; and in such case, if any state shall neglect, then Congress may assess and levy such state's proportion, together with the interest thereon, at the rate of six per cent. per annum, from the time of payment prescribed in such requisition.

V. That Congress shall erect no company of merchants with exclusive advantages of commerce.

VI. That no person shall be tried for any crime by which he may incur an infamous punishment, or loss of life, until he first be indicted by a grand jury, except in such cases as may arise in the government and regulation of the land and naval forces.

VII. All common-law cases between citizens of different states shall be commenced in the common-law courts of the respective states; and no appeal shall be allowed to the federal court, in such cases, unless the sum or value of the thing in controversy amount to three thousand dollars.

VIII. In civil actions between citizens of different states, every issue of fact, arising in actions at common law, shall be tried by jury, if the parties, or either of them, request it.

IX. Congress shall at no time consent that any person, holding an office of trust or profit under the United States, shall accept any title of nobility, or any other title or office, from any king, prince, or foreign state.

X. That no standing army shall be kept up in time of peace, unless with the consent of three fourths of the members of each branch of Congress; nor shall soldiers, in time of peace, be quartered upon private houses, without the consent of the owners.

XI. Congress shall make no laws touching religion, or to infringe the rights of conscience.

XII. Congress shall never disarm any citizen, unless such as are or have been in actual rebellion.

And the Convention do, in the name and in behalf of the people of this state, enjoin it upon their representatives in Congress, at all times until the alterations and provisions aforesaid have been considered agreeably to the fifth article of the said Constitution, to exert all their influence, and use all reasonable and legal methods, to obtain a ratification of the said alterations and provisions, in such manner as is provided in the article.

And that the United States in Congress assembled may have due notice of the assent and ratification of the said Constitution by this Convention, it is Resolved, That the assent and ratification aforesaid be engrossed on parchment, together with the recommendation and injunction aforesaid, and with this resolution; and that John Sullivan, Esq., president of the Convention, and John Langdon, Esq., president of the state, transmit the same, countersigned by the secretary of Convention, and the secretary of state, under their hands and seals, to the United States in Congress assembled.

JOHN SULLIVAN, Pres. of the Conv.

JOHN LANGDON, Pres. of the State."

- Virginia: June 25, 1788 = "WE the Delegates of the people of Virginia, duly elected in pursuance of a recommendation from the General Assembly, and now met in Convention, having fully and freely investigated and discussed the proceedings of the Federal Convention, and being prepared as well as the most mature deliberation hath enabled us, to decide thereon, DO in the name and in behalf of the people of Virginia, declare and make known that the powers granted under the Constitution, being derived from the people of the United States may be resumed by them whensoever the same shall be perverted to their injury or oppression, and that every power not granted thereby remains with them and at their will: that therefore no right of any denomination, can be cancelled, abridged, restrained or modified, by the Congress, by the Senate or House of Representatives acting in any capacity, by the President or any department or officer of the United States, except in those instances in which power is given by the Constitution for those purposes: and that among other essential rights, the liberty of conscience and of the press cannot be cancelled, abridged, restrained or modified by any authority of the United States.

With these impressions, with a solemn appeal to the searcher of hearts for the purity of our intentions, and under the conviction, that, whatsoever imperfections may exist in the Constitution, ought rather to be examined in the mode prescribed therein, than to bring the Union into danger by a delay, with a hope of obtaining amendments previous to the ratification:

We the said Delegates, in the name and in behalf of the people of Virginia, do by these presents assent to, and ratify the Constitution recommended on the seventeenth day of September, one thousand seven hundred and eighty seven, by the Federal Convention for the Government of the United States; hereby announcing to all those whom it may concern, that the said Constitution is binding upon the said People, according to an authentic copy hereto annexed, in the words following:

A copy of the Constitution was included in the ratification document.

On motion, Ordered, That the Secretary of this Convention cause to be engrossed, forthwith, two fair copies of the form of ratification, and of the proposed Constitution of Government, as recommended by the Federal Convention on the seventeenth day of September, one thousand seven hundred and eighty seven.

MR. Wythe reported, from the Committee appointed, such amendments to the proposed Constitution of Government for the United States, as were by them deemed necessary to be recommended to the consideration of the Congress which shall first assemble under the said Constitution, to be acted upon according to the mode prescribed in the fifth article thereof; and he read the same in his place, and afterwards delivered them in at the clerk's table, where the same were again read, and are as followeth:

That there be a Declaration or Bill of Rights asserting and securing from encroachment the essential and unalienable rights of the people in some such manner as the following:

1st.   That there are certain natural rights of which men when they form a social compact cannot deprive or divest their posterity, among which are the enjoyment of life, and liberty, with the means of acquiring, possessing and protecting property, and pursuing and obtaining happiness and safety.

2d.   That all power is naturally vested in, and consequently derived from, the people; that magistrates therefore are their trustees, and agents, and at all times amenable to them.

3d.   That the Government ought to be instituted for the common benefit, protection and security of the people; and that the doctrine of non-resistance against arbitrary power and oppression, is absurd, slavish, and destructive to the good and happiness of mankind.

4th.　That no man or set of men are entitled to exclusive or separate public emoluments or privileges from the community, but in consideration of public services; which not being descendible, neither ought the offices of magistrate, legislator or judge, or any other public office to be hereditary

5th.　That the legislative, executive and judiciary powers of government should be separate and distinct, and that the members of the two first may be restrained from oppression by feeling and participating the public burthens, they should at fixed periods be reduced to a private station, return into the mass of the people; and the vacancies be supplied by certain and regular elections, in which all or any part of the former members to be eligible or ineligible, as the rules of the Constitution of Government, and the laws shall direct.

6th.　That elections of Representatives in the legislature ought to be free and frequent, and all men having sufficient evidence of permanent common interest with, and attachment to the community, ought to have the right of suffrage: and no aid, charge, tax or fee can be set, rated, or levied upon the people without their own consent, or that of their representatives, so elected, nor can they be bound by any law, to which they have not in like manner assented for the public good.

7th.　That all power of suspending laws, or the execution of laws by any authority without the consent of the representatives, of the people in the legislature, is injurious to their rights, and ought not to be exercised.

8th.   That in all capital and criminal prosecutions, a man hath a right to demand the cause and nature of his accusation, to be confronted with the accusers and witnesses, to call for evidence and be allowed counsel in his favor, and to a fair and speedy trial by an impartial jury of his vicinage, without whose unanimous consent he cannot be found guilty (except in the government of the land and naval forces) nor can he be compelled to give evidence against himself.

9th.   That no freeman ought to be taken, imprisoned, or disseized of his freehold, liberties, privileges or franchises, or outlawed or exiled, or in any manner destroyed or deprived of his life, liberty, or property but by the law of the land.

10th.   That every freeman restrained of his liberty is entitled to a remedy to enquire into the lawfulness thereof, and to remove the same, if unlawful, and that such remedy ought not to be denied nor delayed.

11th.   That in controversies respecting property, and in suits between man and man, the ancient trial by jury is one of the greatest securities to the rights of the people, and ought to remain sacred and inviolable.

12th.   That every freeman ought to find a certain remedy by recourse to the laws for all injuries and wrongs he may receive in his person, property, or character. He ought to obtain right and justice freely without sale, completely and without denial, promptly and without delay, and that all establishments, or regulations contravening these rights, are oppressive and unjust.

13th.   That excessive bail ought not to be required, nor excessive fines imposed, nor cruel and unusual punishments inflicted.

14th. That every freeman has a right to be secure from all unreasonable searches, and seizures of his person, his papers, and property; all warrants therefore to search suspected places, or seize any freeman, his papers or property, without information upon oath (or affirmation of a person religiously scrupulous of taking an oath) of legal and sufficient cause, are grievous and oppressive, and all general warrants to search suspected places, or to apprehend any suspected person without specially naming or describing the place or person, are dangerous and ought not to be granted.

15th. That the people have a right peaceably to assemble together to consult for the common good, or to instruct their representatives; and that every freeman has a right to petition or apply to the Legislature for redress of grievances.

16th. That the people have a right to freedom of speech, and of writing and publishing their sentiments; that the freedom of the press is one of the greatest bulwarks of liberty, and ought not to be violated.

17th. That the people have a right to keep and bear arms; that a well regulated militia composed of the body of the people trained to arms, is the proper, natural and safe defence of a free state. That standing armies in time of peace are dangerous to liberty, and therefore ought to be avoided, as far as the circumstances and protection of the community will admit; and that in all cases, the military should be under strict subordination to and governed by the civil power.

18th. That no soldier in time of peace ought to be quartered in any house without the consent of the owner, and in time of war in such manner only as the laws direct.

19th.   That any person religiously scrupulous of bearing arms ought to be exempted upon payment of an equivalent to employ another to bear arms in his stead.

20th.   That religion, or the duty which we owe to our Creator, and the manner of discharging it, can be directed only by reason and conviction, not by force or violence, and therefore all men have an equal, natural and unalienable right to the exercise of religion according to the dictates of conscience, and that no particular sect or society ought to be favored or established by law in preference to others.

AMENDMENTS TO THE Constitution.

1st.   That each state in the union shall respectively retain every power, jurisdiction and right, which is not by this Constitution delegated to the Congress of the United States, or to the departments of the Federal Government.

2d.   That there shall be one representative for every thirty thousand, according to the enumeration or census mentioned in the Constitution, until the whole number of representatives amounts to two hundred; after which that number shall be continued or increased as Congress shall direct, upon the principles fixed in the Constitution, by apportioning the representatives of each state to some greater number of people from time to time as population increases.

3d.   When Congress shall lay direct taxes or excises, they shall immediately inform the executive power of each state, of the quota of such state according to the census herein directed, which is proposed to be thereby raised; and if the legislature of any state shall pass a law which shall be effectual for raising such quota at the time required by Congress, the taxes and excises laid by Congress, shall not be collected in such state.

4th.   That the members of the Senate and House of Representatives shall be ineligible to, and incapable of holding any civil office under the authority of the United States, during the time for which they shall respectively be elected.

5th.   That the journals of the proceedings of the Senate and House of Representatives shall be published at least once in every year, except such parts thereof relating to treaties, alliances, or military operations, as in their judgment require secrecy.

6th.   That a regular statement and account of the receipts and expenditures of all public money, shall be published at least once in every year.

7th.   That no commercial treaty shall be ratified without the concurrence of two thirds of the whole number of the members of the Senate; and no treaty, ceding, contracting, or restraining or suspending the territorial rights or claims of the United States, or any of them, or their, or any of their rights or claims to fishing in the American seas, or navigating the American rivers, shall be made, but in cases of the most urgent and extreme necessity, nor shall any such treaty be ratified without the concurrence of three fourths of the whole number of the members of both houses respectively.

8th.   That no navigation law or law regulating commerce shall be passed without the consent of two thirds of the members present, in both houses.

9th.   That no standing army or regular troops shall be raised, or kept up in time of peace, without the consent of two thirds of the members present, in both houses.

10th.   That no soldier shall be inlisted for any longer term than four years, except in time of war, and then for no longer term than the continuance of the war.

11th.   That each state respectively shall have the power to provide for organizing, arming and disciplining its own militia, whensoever Congress shall omit or neglect to provide for the same. That the militia shall not be subject to martial law, except when in actual service in time of war, invasion or rebellion, and when not in the actual service of the United States, shall be subject only to such fines, penalties and punishments as shall be directed or inflicted by the laws of its own state.

12th.   That the exclusive power of legislation given to Congress over the Federal Town and its adjacent district, and other places purchased or to be purchased by Congress of any of the states, shall extend only to such regulations as respect the police and good government thereof.

13th.   That no person shall be capable of being President of the United States for more than eight years in any term of sixteen years.

14th.   That the judicial power of the United States shall be vested in one Supreme Court, and in such Courts of Admiralty as Congress may from time to time ordain and establish in any of the different states: The judicial power shall extend to all cases in law and equity arising under treaties made, or which shall be made under the authority of the United States; to all cases affecting ambassadors, other foreign ministers and consuls; to all cases of admiralty and maritime jurisdiction; to controversies to which the United States shall be a party; to controversies between two or more States, and between parties claiming lands under the grants of different States. In all cases affecting ambassadors, other foreign ministers and consuls, and those in which a state shall be a party, the Supreme Court shall have original jurisdiction; in all other cases before mentioned, the Supreme Court shall have appellate jurisdiction, as to matters of law only: except in cases of equity, and of admiralty and maritime jurisdiction, in which the Supreme Court shall have a appellate jurisdiction both as to law and fact, with such exceptions and under such regulations as the Congress shall make: But the judicial power of the United States shall extend to no case where the cause of action shall have originated before the ratification of this Constitution; except in disputes between States about their territory; disputes between persons claiming lands under the grants of different States, and suits for debts due to the United States.

15th.   That in criminal prosecutions, no man shall be restrained in the exercise of the usual and accustomed right of challenging or excepting to the jury.

16th.   That Congress shall not alter, modify, or interfere in the times, places, or manner of holding elections for Senators and Representatives, or either of them, except when the Legislature of any state shall neglect, refuse, or be disabled by invasion or rebellion to prescribe the same.

17th.   That those clauses which declare that Congress shall not exercise certain powers, be not interpreted in any manner whatsoever, to extend the powers of Congress; but that they be construed either as making exceptions to the specified powers where this shall be the case, or otherwise, as inserted merely for greater caution.

18th.   That the laws ascertaining the compensation of Senators and representatives for their services, be postponed in their operation, until after the election of representatives immediately succeeding the passing thereof; that excepted, which shall first be passed on the subject.

19th.   That some tribunal other than the Senate be provided for trying impeachments of Senators.

20th.   That the salary of a judge shall not be increased or diminished during his continuance in office otherwise than by general regulations of salary, which may take place on a revision of the subject at stated periods of not less than seven years, to commence from the same such salaries shall be first ascertained by Congress.

AND the Convention do, in the name and behalf of the people of this Commonwealth, enjoin it upon their representatives in Congress to exert all their influence and use all reasonable and legal methods to obtain a RATIFICATION of the foregoing alterations and provisions in the manner provided by the fifth article of the said Constitution; and in all Congressional laws to be passed in the meantime, to conform to the spirit of these amendments as far as the said Constitution will admit."

- New York: July 26, 1788 = "We, the delegates of the people of the state of New York, duly elected and met in Convention, having maturely considered the Constitution for the United

States of America, agreed to on the 17th day of September, in the year 1787, by the Convention then assembled at Philadelphia, in the commonwealth of Pennsylvania, (a copy whereof precedes these presents,) and having also seriously and deliberately considered the present situation of the United States, — Do declare and make known, —

That all power is originally vested in, and consequently derived from, the people, and that government is instituted by them for their common interest, protection, and security.

That the enjoyment of life, liberty, and the pursuit of happiness, are essential rights, which every government ought to respect and preserve.

That the powers of government may be reassumed by the people whensoever it shall become necessary to their happiness; that every power, jurisdiction, and right, which is not by the said Constitution clearly delegated to the Congress of the United States, or the departments of the government thereof, remains to the people of the several states, or to their respective state governments, to whom they may have granted the same; and that those clauses in the said Constitution, which declare that Congress shall not have or exercise certain powers, do not imply that Congress is entitled to any powers not given by the said Constitution; but such clauses are to be construed either as exceptions to certain specified powers, or as inserted merely for greater caution.

That the people have an equal, natural, and unalienable right freely and peaceably to exercise their religion, according to the dictates of conscience; and that no religious sect or society ought to be favored or established by law in preference to others.

That the people have a right to keep and bear arms; that a well-regulated militia, including the body of the people capable of bearing arms, is the proper, natural, and safe defence of a free state.

That the militia should not be subject to martial law, except in time of war, rebellion, or insurrection.

That standing armies, in time of peace, are dangerous to liberty, and ought not to be kept up, except in cases of necessity; and that at all times the military should be under strict subordination to the civil power.

That, in time of peace, no soldier ought to be quartered in any house without the consent of the owner, and in time of war only by the civil magistrate, in such manner as the laws may direct.

That no person ought to be taken, imprisoned, or disseized of his freehold, or be exiled, or deprived of his privileges, franchises, life, liberty, or property, but by due process of law.

That no person ought to be put twice in jeopardy of life or limb, for one and the same offence; nor, unless in case of impeachment, be punished more than once for the same offence.

That every person restrained of his liberty is entitled to an inquiry into the lawfulness of such restraint, and to a removal thereof if unlawful; and that such inquiry or removal ought not to be denied or delayed, except when, on account of public danger, the Congress shall suspend the privilege of the writ of habeas corpus.

That excessive bail ought not to be required, nor excessive fines imposed, nor cruel or unusual punishments inflicted.

That (except in the government of the land and naval forces, and of the militia when in actual service, and in cases of impeachment) a presentment or indictment by a grand jury ought to be observed as a necessary preliminary to the trial of all crimes cognizable by the judiciary of the United States; and such trial should be speedy, public, and by an impartial jury of the county where the crime was committed; and that no person can be found guilty without the unanimous consent of such jury. But in cases of crimes not committed within any county of any of the United States, and in cases of crimes committed within any county in which a general insurrection may prevail, or which may be in the possession of a foreign enemy, the inquiry and trial may be in such county as the Congress shall by law direct; which county, in the two cases last mentioned, should be as near as conveniently may be to that county in which the crime may have been committed; — and that, in all criminal prosecutions, the accused ought to be informed of the cause and nature of his accusation, to be confronted with his accusers and the witnesses against him, to have the means of producing his witnesses, and the assistance of counsel for his defence; and should not be compelled to give evidence against himself.

That the trial by jury, in the extent that it obtains by the common law of England, is one of the greatest securities to the rights of a free people, and ought to remain inviolate.

That every freeman has a right to be secure from all unreasonable searches and seizures of his person, his papers, or his property; and therefore, that all warrants to search suspected places, or seize any freeman, his papers, or property, without information, upon oath or affirmation, of sufficient cause, are grievous and oppressive; and that all general warrants (or such in which the place or person suspected are not particularly designated) are dangerous, and ought not to be granted.

That the people have a right peaceably to assemble together to consult for their common good, or to instruct their representatives, and that every person has a right to petition or apply to the legislature for redress of grievances.

That the freedom of the press ought not to be violated or restrained.

That there should be, once in four years, an election of the President and Vice-President, so that no officer, who may be appointed by the Congress to act as President, in case of the removal, death, resignation, or inability, of the President and Vice-President, can in any case continue to act beyond the termination of the period for which the last President and Vice-President were elected.

That nothing contained in the said Constitution is to be construed to prevent the legislature of any state from passing laws at its discretion, from time to time, to divide such state into convenient districts, and to apportion its representatives to and amongst such districts.

That the prohibition contained in the said Constitution, against ex post facto laws, extends only to laws concerning crimes.

That all appeals in causes determinable according to the course of the common law, ought to be by writ of error, and not otherwise.

That the judicial power of the United States, in cases in which a state may be a party, does not extend to criminal prosecutions, or to authorize any suit by any person against a state.

That the judicial power of the United States, as to controversies between citizens of the same state, claiming lands under grants from different states, is not to be construed to extend to any other controversies between them, except those which relate to such lands, so claimed, under grants of different states.

That the jurisdiction of the Supreme Court of the United States, or of any other court to be instituted by the Congress, is not in any case to be increased, enlarged, or extended, by any faction, collusion, or mere suggestion; and that no treaty is to be construed so to operate as to alter the Constitution of any state.

Under these impressions, and declaring that the rights aforesaid cannot be abridged or violated, and that the explanations aforesaid are consistent with the said Constitution, and in confidence that the amendments which shall have been proposed to the said Constitution will receive an early and mature consideration, — We, the said delegates, in the name and in the behalf of the people of the state of New York, do, by these presents, assent to and ratify the said Constitution. In full confidence, nevertheless, that, until a convention shall be called and convened for proposing amendments to the said Constitution, the militia of this state will not be continued in service out of this state for a longer term than six weeks, without the consent of the legislature thereof; that the Congress will not make or alter any regulation in this state, respecting the times, places, and manner, of holding elections for senators or representatives, unless the legislature of this state shall neglect or refuse to make laws or regulations for the purpose, or from any circumstance be incapable of making the same; and that, in those cases, such power will only be exercised until the legislature of this state shall make provision in the premises; that no excise will be imposed on any article of the growth, production, or manufacture of the United States, or any of them, within this state, ardent spirits excepted; and the Congress will not lay direct taxes within this state, but when the moneys arising from the impost and excise shall be insufficient for the public exigencies, nor then, until Congress shall first have made a requisition upon this state to assess, levy, and pay, the amount of such requisition, made agreeably to the census fixed in the said Constitution, in such way and manner as the legislature of this state shall judge best; but that in such case, if the state shall neglect or refuse to pay its proportion, pursuant to such requisition, then the Congress may assess and levy this state's proportion, together with interest, at the rate of six per centum per annum, from the time at which the same was required to be paid.

Done in Convention, at Poughkeepsie, in the county of Duchess, in the state of New York, the 26th day of July, in the year of our Lord 1788.

By order of the Convention.GEO. CLINTON, President.

Attested. John M'Kesson, A. B. Banker, Secretaries.

And the Convention do, in the name and behalf of the people of the state of New York, enjoin it upon their representatives in Congress to exert all their influence, and use all reasonable means, to obtain a ratification of the following amendments to the said Constitution, in the manner prescribed therein; and in all laws to be passed by the Congress, in the mean time, to conform to the spirit of the said amendments, as far as the Constitution will admit.

That there shall be one representatives for every thirty thousand inhabitants, according to the enumeration or census mentioned in the Constitution, until the whole number of representatives amounts to two hundred, after which that number shall be continued or increased, but not diminished, as the Congress shall direct, and according to such ratio as the Congress shall fix, in conformity to the rule prescribed for the apportionment of representatives and direct taxes.

That the Congress do not impose any excise on any article (ardent spirits excepted) of the growth, production, or manufacture of the United States, or any of them.

That Congress do not lay direct taxes but when the moneys arising from the impost and excise shall be insufficient for the public exigencies, nor then, until Congress shall first have made a requisition upon the states to assess, levy, and pay, their respective proportions of such requisition, agreeably to the census fixed in the said Constitution, in such way and manner as the legislatures of the respective states shall judge best; and in such case, if any state shall neglect or refuse to pay its proportion, pursuant to such requisition, then Congress may assess and levy such state's proportion, together with interest at the rate of six per centum per annum, from the time of payment prescribed in such requisition.

That the Congress shall not make or alter any regulation, in any state, respecting the times, places, and manner, of holding elections for senators and representatives, unless the legislature of such state shall neglect or refuse to make laws or regulations for the purpose, or from any circumstance be incapable of making the same, and then only until the legislature of such state shall make provision in the premises; provided, that Congress may prescribe the time for the election of representatives.

That no persons, except natural-born citizens, or such as were citizens on or before the 4th day of July, 1776, or such as held commissions under the United States during the war, and have at any time since the 4th day of July, 1776, become citizens of one or other of the United States, and who shall be freeholders, shall be eligible to the places of President, Vice-President, or members of either house of the Congress of the United States.

That the Congress do not grant monopolies, or erect any company with exclusive advantages of commerce.

That no standing army or regular troops shall be raised, or kept up, in time of peace, without the consent of two thirds of the senators and representatives present in each house.

That no money be borrowed on the credit of the United States without the assent of two thirds of the senators and representatives present in each house.

That the Congress shall not declare war without the concurrence of two thirds of the senators and representatives present in each house. That the privilege of the habeas corpus shall not, by any law, be suspended for a longer term than six months, or until twenty days after the meeting of the Congress next following the passing the act for such suspension.

That the right of Congress to exercise exclusive legislation over such district, not exceeding ten miles square, as may, by cession of a particular state, and the acceptance of Congress, become the seat of government of the United States, shall not be so exercised as to exempt the inhabitants of such district from paying the like taxes, imposts, duties, and excises, as shall be imposed on the other inhabitants of the state in which such district may be; and that no person shall be privileged within the said district from arrest for crimes committed, or debts contracted, out of the said district.

That the right of exclusive legislation, with respect to such places as may be purchased for the erection of forts, magazines, arsenals, dock-yards, and other needful buildings, shall not authorize the Congress to make any law to prevent the laws of the states, respectively, in which they may be, from extending to such places in all civil and criminal matters, except as to such persons as shall be in the service of the United States; nor to them with respect to crimes committed without such places.

That the compensation for the senators and representatives be ascertained by standing laws; and that no alteration of the existing rate of compensation shall operate for the benefit of the representatives until after a subsequent election shall have been had.

That the Journals of the Congress shall be published at least once a year, with the exception of such parts, relating to treaties or military operations, as, in the judgment of either house, shall require secrecy; and that both houses of Congress shall always keep their doors open during their sessions, unless the business may, in their opinion, require secrecy. That the yeas and nays shall be entered on the Journals whenever two members in either house may require it.

That no capitation tax shall ever be laid by Congress.

That no person be eligible as a senator for more than six years in any term of twelve years; and that the legislatures of the respective states may recall their senators, or either of them, and elect others in their stead, to serve the remainder of the time for which the senators so recalled were appointed.

That no senator or representative shall, during the time for which he was elected, be appointed to any office under the authority of the United States.

That the authority given to the executives of the states to fill up the vacancies of senators be abolished, and that such vacancies be filled by the respective legislatures.

That the power of Congress to pass uniform laws concerning bankruptcy shall only extend to merchants and other traders; and the states, respectively, may pass laws for the relief of other insolvent debtors.

That no person shall be eligible to the office of President of the United States a third time.

That the executive shall not grant pardons for treason, unless with the consent of the Congress; but may, at his discretion, grant reprieves to persons convicted of treason, until their cases can be laid before the Congress.

That the President, or person exercising his powers for the time being, shall not command an army in the field in person, without the previous desire of the Congress.

That all letters patent, commissions, pardons, writs, and processes of the United States, shall run in the name of the people of the United States, and be tested in the name of the President of the United States, or the person exercising his powers for the time being, or the first judge of the court out of which the same, shall issue, as the case may be.

That the Congress shall not constitute, ordain, or establish, any tribunals of inferior courts, with any other than appellate jurisdiction, except such as may be necessary for the trial of cases of admiralty and maritime jurisdiction, and for the trial of piracies and felonies committed on the high seas; and in all other cases to which the judicial power of the United States extends, and in which the Supreme Court of the United States has not original jurisdiction, the causes shall be heard, tried, and determined, in some one of the state courts, with the right of appeal to the Supreme Court of the United States, or other proper tribunal, to be established for that purpose by the Congress, with such exceptions, and under such regulations, as the Congress shall make.

That the court for the trial of impeachments shall consist of the Senate, the judges of the Supreme Court of the United States, and the first or senior judge, for the time being, of the highest court of general and ordinary common- law jurisdiction in each state; that the Congress shall, by standing laws, designate the courts in the respective states answering this description, and, in states having no courts exactly answering this description, shall designate some other court, preferring such, if any there be, whose judge or judges may hold their places during good behavior; provided, that no more than one judge, other than judges of the Supreme Court of the United States, shall come from one state.

That the Congress be authorized to pass laws for compensating the judges for such services, and for compelling their attendance; and that a majority, at least, of the said judges shall be requisite to constitute the said court. That no person impeached shall sit as a member thereof; that each member shall, previous to the entering upon any trial, take an oath or affirmation honestly and impartially to hear and determine the cause; and that a majority of the members present shall be necessary to a conviction.

That persons aggrieved by any judgment, sentence, or decree, of the Supreme Court of the United States, in any cause in which that court has original jurisdiction, with such exceptions, and under such regulations, as the Congress shall make concerning the same, shall, upon application, have a commission, to be issued by the President of the United States to such men learned in the law as he shall nominate, and by and with the advice and consent of the Senate appoint, not less than seven, authorizing such commissioners, or any seven or more of them, to correct the errors in such judgment, or to review such sentence and decree, as the case may be, and to do justice to the parties in the premises.

That no judge of the Supreme Court of the United States shall hold any other office under the United States, or any of them.
That the judicial power of the United States shall extend to no controversies respecting land, unless it relate to claims of territory or jurisdiction between states, and individuals under the grants of different states.

That the militia of any state shall not be compelled to serve without the limits of the state, for a longer term than six weeks, without the consent of the legislature thereof.

That the words without the consent of the Congress, in the seventh clause of the ninth section of the first article of the Constitution, be expunged.

That the senators and representatives, and all executive and judicial officers of the United States, shall be bound by oath or affirmation not to infringe or violate the Constitutions or rights of the respective states.

That the legislatures of the respective states may make provision, by law, that the electors of the election districts, to be by them appointed, shall choose a citizen of the United States, who shall have been an inhabitant of such district for the term of one year immediately preceding the time of his election, for one the representatives of such state.

Done in Convention, at Poughkeepsie, in the county of Duchess, in the state of New York, the 26th day of July, in the year of our Lord 1788.

- North Carolina: November 21, 1789 = "In Convention.

Whereas the General Convention which met in Philadelphia, in pursuance of a recommendation of Congress, did recommend to the citizens of the United States a Constitution or form of government in the following words, namely, —

(A copy of the Constitution was included in the ratification document.)

Resolved, That this Convention, in behalf of the freemen, citizens and inhabitants of the state of North Carolina, do adopt and ratify the said Constitution and form of government.

Done in Convention this twenty-first day of November, one thousand seven hundred and eighty-nine.

SAMUEL JOHNSON,

President of the Convention.

J. Hunt, James Taylor, Secretaries.

Resolved, That a declaration of rights, asserting and securing from encroachment the great principles of civil and religious liberty, and the unalienable rights of the people, together with amendments to the most ambiguous and exceptionable parts of the said Constitution of government, ought to be laid before Congress, and the convention of the states that shall or may be called for the purpose of amending the said Constitution, for their consideration, previous to the ratification of the Constitution aforesaid on the part of the state of North Carolina.

DECLARATION OF RIGHTS.

1. That there are certain natural rights, of which men, when they form a social compact, cannot deprive or divest their posterity, among which are the enjoyment of life and liberty, with the means of acquiring, possessing, and protecting property, and pursuing and obtaining happiness and safety.

2. That all power is naturally vested in, and consequently derived from, the people; that magistrates, therefore, are their trustees and

agents, and at all times amenable to them.

3.   That government ought to be instituted for the common benefit, protection, and security, of the people; and that the doctrine of non-resistance against arbitrary power and oppression is absurd, slavish, and destructive to the good and happiness of mankind.

4.   That no man or set of men are entitled to exclusive or separate public emoluments or privileges from the community, but in consideration of public services, which not being descendible, neither ought the offices of magistrate, legislator, or judge, or any other public office to be hereditary.

5.   That the legislative, executive, and judiciary powers of government should be separate and distinct, and that the members of the two first may be restrained from oppression by feeling and participating the public burdens: they should, at fixed periods, be reduced to a private station, return into the mass of the people, and the vacancies be supplied by certain and regular elections, in which all or any part of the former members to be eligible or ineligible, as the rules of the Constitution of government and the laws shall direct.

6.   That elections of representatives in the legislature ought to be free and frequent, and all men having sufficient evidence of permanent common interest with, and attachment to, the community, ought to have the right of suffrage; and no aid, charge, tax, or fee, can be set, rated, or levied, upon the people without their own consent, or that of their representatives so elected; nor can they be bound by any law to which they have not in like manner assented for the public good.

7.   That all power of suspending laws, or the execution of laws, by any authority, without the consent of the representatives of the people in the legislature, is injurious to their rights, and ought not to be exercised.

8.   That, in all capital and criminal prosecutions, a man hath a right to demand the cause and nature of his accusation, to be confronted with the accusers and witnesses, to call for evidence, and be allowed counsel in his favor, and a fair and speedy trial by an impartial jury of his vicinage, without whose unanimous consent he cannot be found guilty, (except in the government of the land and naval forces;) nor can he be compelled to give evidence against himself.

9.   That no freeman ought to be taken, imprisoned, or disseized of his freehold, liberties, privileges, or franchises, or outlawed or exiled, or in any manner destroyed, or deprived of his life, liberty, or property, but by the law of the land.

10. That every freeman, restrained of his liberty, is entitled to a remedy to inquire into the lawfulness thereof, and to remove the same if unlawful; and that such remedy ought not to be denied nor delayed.

11. That, in controversies respecting property, and in suits between man and man, the ancient trial by jury is one of the greatest securities to the rights of the people, and ought to remain sacred and inviolable.

12. That every freeman ought to find a certain remedy, by recourse to the laws, for all injuries and wrongs he may receive in his person, property,or character; he ought to obtain right and justice freely without sale, completely and without denial, promptly and without delay; and that all establishments or regulations contravening these

rights are oppressive and unjust.

13. That excessive bail ought not to be required, nor excessive fines imposed, nor cruel and unusual punishments inflicted.

14. That every freeman has a right to be secure from all unreasonable searches and seizures of his person, his papers and property; all warrants; therefore, to search suspected places, or to apprehend any suspected person, without specially naming or describing the place or person, are dangerous, and ought not to be granted.

15. That the people have a right peaceably to assemble together, to consult for the common good, or to instruct their representatives; and that every freeman has a right to petition or apply to the legislature for redress of grievances.

16. That the people have a right to freedom of speech, and of writing and publishing their sentiments that freedom of the press is one of the greatest bulwarks of liberty, and ought not to be violated.

17. That the people have a right to keep and bear arms; that a well-regulated militia, composed of the body of the people, trained to arms, is the proper, natural, and safe defence of a free state; that standing armies, in time of peace, are dangerous to liberty, and therefore ought to be avoided, as far as the circumstances and protection of the community will admit; and that. in all cases, the military should be under strict subordination to, and governed by, the civil power.

18. That no soldier, in time of peace, ought to be quartered in any house Without the consent of the owner, and in time of war, in such manner only as the laws direct.

19. That any person religiously scrupulous of bearing arms ought to be exempted, upon payment of an equivalent to employ another to bear arms in his stead.

20. That religion, or the duty which we owe to our Creator, and the manner of discharging it, can be directed only by reason and conviction, not by force or violence: and therefore all men have an equal, natural, and unalienable right to the free exercise of religion, according to the dictates of conscience; and that no particular religious sect or society ought to be favored or established by law in preference to others.

AMENDMENTS TO THE CONSTITUTION.

1. That each state in the Union shall respectively retain every power, jurisdiction, and right, which is not by this Constitution delegated to the Congress of the United States, or to the departments of the federal government.

2. That there shall be one representative for every thirty thousand, according to the, enumeration or census mentioned in the Constitution, until the Whole number of representatives amounts to two hundred; after which that number shall be continued or increased as Congress shall direct, upon the principles fixed in the Constitution, by apportioning the representatives of each state to some greater number of the people; from time to time, as the population increases.

3. When Congress shall lay direct taxes or excises, they shall, immediately inform the executive power of each state of the quota of such state, according to the census herein directed, which is proposed to be thereby raised; and if the legislature of any state shall pass

any law. which shall be effectual for raising such quota at the time required by Congress, the taxes and excises laid by Congress shall not be collected in such state.

4. That the members of the Senate and House of Representatives shall be ineligible to, and incapable of holding, any civil office under the authority of the United States, during the time for which they shall respectively be elected.

5. That the Journals of the proceedings of the Senate and House of Representatives shall be published at least once in every year, except such parts thereof relating to treaties, alliances, or military operations, as in their judgment require secrecy.

6. That a regular statement and account of receipts and expenditures of all public moneys shall be published at least once in every year.

7. That no commercial treaty shall be ratified without the concurrence of two thirds of the whole number of the members of the Senate. And no treaty, ceding, contracting, restraining, or suspending, the territorial rights or claims of the United States, or any of them, or their, or any of their, rights or claims of fishing in the American seas, or navigating the American rivers, shall be made, but in cases of the most urgent and extreme necessity; nor shall any such treaty be ratified without the concurrence of three fourths of the whole number of the members of both houses respectively.

8. That no navigation law, or law regulating commerce, shall be passed without the consent of two thirds of the members present in both houses.

9.   That no standing army or regular troops shall be raised or kept up in time of peace, without the consent of two thirds of the members present in both houses.

10. That no soldier shall be enlisted for any longer term than four years, except in time of war, and then for no longer term than the continuance of the war.

11. That each state respectively shall have the power to provide for organizing, arming, and disciplining its own militia; whensoever: Congress shall omit or neglect to provide for the same; that the militia shall not be subject to martial law, except when in actual service in time of war, invasion, or rebellion; and when not in the actual service of the United States, shall be subject only to such fines, penalties, and punishments, as shall be directed or inflicted by the laws of its own state.

12. That Congress shall not declare any state to be in rebellion, without the consent of at least two thirds of all the members present, in both houses.

13. That the exclusive power of legislation given to Congress Over the federal town and its adjacent district, and other places purchased or to be purchased by Congress of any of the states, shall extend only to such regulations as respect the police and good government thereof.

14. That no person shall be capable of being President of the United States for more than eight years in any term of fifteen years.

15. That the judicial power of the United States shall be vested in one. Supreme Court, and in such courts of admiralty as Congress may

from time to time ordain and establish in any of the different states. The judicial power shall extend to all cases in law and equity arising under treaties made, or which shall be made, under the authority of the United States; to all cases affecting ambassadors, other foreign ministers, and consuls; to all cases of admiralty and maritime jurisdiction; to controversies to which the united States shall be a party; to controversies between two or more states, and between parties claiming lauds under the grants of different states. In all cases affecting ambassadors, other foreign ministers, and consuls, and those in which a state shall be a party, the Supreme Court shall have original jurisdiction. In all other cases before mentioned, the Supreme Court shall have appellate jurisdiction as to matters of law only, except in eases of equity, and of admiralty and maritime jurisdiction, in which the Supreme Court shall have appellate jurisdiction both as to law and fact, with such exceptions, and under such regulations, as the Congress shall make: but the judicial power of the United States shall extend to no case where the cause of action shall have originated before the ratification of this Constitution, except in disputes between states about their territory, disputes between persons claiming lands under the grants of different, states, and suits for debts due to the United States.

16. That, in criminal prosecutions, no man shall be restrained in the exercise of the usual and accustomed tight of challenging or excepting to the jury.

17. That Congress shall not alter, modify, or interfere in, the times, places, or manner, of holding elections for senators and representatives, or either of them, except when the legislature of any state shall neglect, refuse, or be disabled, by invasion or rebellion, to prescribe the same.

18. That those clauses which declare that Congress shall not exercise certain powers he not interpreted in any manner whatsoever to extend the power of Congress; but that they be construed either as making exceptions to the specified powers where this shall be the case, or otherwise as inserted merely for greater caution.

19. That the laws ascertaining the compensation of senators and representatives for their services, be postponed in their operation until after the election of representatives immediately succeeding the passing thereof, that excepted which shall first be passed on the subject.

20. That some tribunal other than the Senate be provided for trying impeachments of senators.

21. That the salary of a judged shall not be increased or diminished during his continuance in office, otherwise than by general regulations of salary, which may take place on a revision of the subject at stated periods of not less than seven years, to commence froth the time such salaries shall be first ascertained by Congress.

22. That Congress erect no company of merchants with exclusive advantages of commerce.

23. That no treaties which shall be directly opposed to the existing laws of the United States in Congress assembled shall be valid until such laws shall be repealed, or made conformable to such treaty; nor shall any treaty be valid which is contradictory to the Constitution of the United States.

24. What the latter part of the 5th paragraph of the 9th section of the 1st article be altered to read thus: 'Nor shall vessels hound to a particular state be obliged to enter or pay duties in any other; nor, when bound from any one of the states, be obliged to clear in another.'

25. That Congress shall not, directly or indirectly; either by themselves or through the judiciary, interfere with any one of the states in the redemption of paper money already emitted and now in circulation, or in liquidating and discharging the public securities of any one of the states; but each and every state shall have the exclusive right of making such laws and regulations, for the above purposes, as they shall think proper.

26. That Congress shall not introduce foreign troops into the United States without the consent of two thirds of the members present of both houses."

• Rhode Island: May 29, 1790 (Rhode Island did not attend the Constitutional Convention. A copy of the Constitution was included in the ratification document.)

Ratification of the Constitution by the Convention of the State of Rhode Island and Providence Plantations.

We, the delegates of the people of the state of Rhode Island and Providence Plantations, duly elected and met in Convention, having maturely considered the Constitution for the United States of America, agreed to on the seventeenth day of September, in the year one thousand seven hundred and eighty-seven, by the Convention then assembled at Philadelphia, in the commonwealth of Pennsylvania, (a copy whereof precedes these presents,) and having also seriously and deliberately considered the present situation of this state, do declare and make known,—

I. That there are certain natural rights of which men, when they form a social compact, cannot deprive or divest their posterity,— among which are the enjoyment of life and liberty, with the means of acquiring, possessing, and protecting property, and pursuing and obtaining happiness and safety.

II. That all power is naturally vested in, and consequently derived from, the people; that magistrates, therefore, are their trustees and agents, and at all times amenable to them.

III. That the powers of government may be reassumed by the people whensoever it shall become necessary to their happiness. That the rights of the states respectively to nominate and appoint all state officers, and every other power, jurisdiction, and right, which is not by the said Constitution clearly delegated to the Congress of the United States, or to the departments of government thereof, remain to the people of the several states, or their respective state governments, to whom they may have granted the same; and that those clauses in the Constitution which declare that Congress shall not have or exercise certain powers, do not imply that Congress is entitled to any powers not given by the said Constitution; but such clauses are to be construed as exceptions to certain specified powers, or as inserted merely for greater caution.

IV. That religion, or the duty which we owe to our Creator, and the manner of discharging it, can be directed only by reason and conviction, and not by force and violence; and therefore all men have a natural, equal, and unalienable right to the exercise of religion according to the dictates of conscience; and that no particular religious sect or society ought to be favored or established, by law, in preference to others.

V. That the legislative, executive, and judiciary powers of government should be separate and distinct; and, that the members of the two first may be restrained from oppression, by feeling and participating the public burdens, they should, at fixed periods, be reduced to a private station, returned into the mass of the people, and the vacancies be supplied by certain and regular elections, in which all or any part of the former members to be eligible or ineligible, as the rules of the Constitution of government and the laws shall direct.

VI. That elections of representatives in legislature ought to be free and frequent; and all men having sufficient evidence of permanent common interest with, and attachment to, the community, ought to have the right of suffrage; and no aid, charge, tax, or fee, can be set, rated, or levied, upon the people without their own consent, or that of their representatives so elected, nor can they be bound by any law to which they have not in like manner consented for the public good.

VII. That all power of suspending laws, or the execution of laws, by any authority, without the consent of the representatives of the people in the legislature, is injurious to their rights, and ought not to be exercised.

VIII. That, in all capital and criminal prosecutions, a man hath the right to demand the cause and nature of his accusation, to be confronted with the accusers and witnesses, to call for evidence, and be allowed counsel in his favor, and to a fair and speedy trial by an impartial jury in his vicinage, without whose unanimous consent he cannot be found guilty, (except in the government of the land and naval forces,) nor can he be compelled to give evidence against himself.

IX.   That no freeman ought to be taken, imprisoned, or disseized of his freehold, liberties, privileges, or franchises, or outlawed, or exiled, or in any manner destroyed or deprived of his life, liberty or property, but by the trial by jury, or by the law of the land.

X. That every freeman restrained of his liberty is entitled to a remedy, to inquire into the lawfulness thereof, and to remove the same if unlawful, and that such remedy ought not to be denied or delayed.

XI.   That in controversies respecting property, and in suits between man and man, the ancient trial by jury, as hath been exercised by us and our ancestors, from the time whereof the memory of man is not to the contrary, is one of the greatest securities to the rights of the people, and ought to remain sacred and inviolable.

XII. That every freeman ought to obtain right and justice, freely and without sale completely and without denial, promptly and without delay; and that all establishments or regulations contravening these rights are oppressive and unjust.

XIII. That excessive bail ought not to be required, nor excessive fines imposed, nor cruel or unusual punishments inflicted.

XIV.   That every person has a right to be secure from all unreasonable searches and seizures of his person his papers, or his property; and therefore, that all warrants to search suspected places, to seize any person, his papers, or his property, without information upon oath or affirmation of sufficient cause, are grievous and oppressive; and that all general warrants (or such in which the place or person suspected are not particularly designated) are dangerous, and ought not to be granted.

XV. That the people have a right peaceably to assemble together to consult for their common good, or to instruct their representatives; and that every person has a right to petition or apply to the legislature for redress of grievances.

XVI. That the people have a right to freedom of speech, and of writing and publishing their sentiments. That freedom of the press is one of the greatest bulwarks of liberty, and ought not to be violated.

XVII. That the people have a right to keep and bear arms; that a well- regulated militia, including the body of the people capable of bearing arms, is the proper, natural, and safe defence of a free state; that the militia shall not be subject to martial law, except in time of war, rebellion, or insurrection; that standing armies, in time of peace, are dangerous to liberty, and ought not to be kept up, except in cases of necessity; and that, at all times, the military should be under strict subordination to the civil power; that, in time of peace, no soldier ought to be quartered in any house without the consent of the owner, and in time of war only by the civil magistrates, in such manner as the law directs.

XVIII. That any person religiously scrupulous of bearing arms ought to be exempted upon payment of an equivalent to employ another to bear arms in his stead.

Under these impressions, and declaring that the rights aforesaid cannot be abridged or violated, and that the explanations aforesaid are consistent with the said Constitution, and in confidence that the amendments hereafter mentioned will receive an early and mature consideration, and, conformably to the fifth article of said Constitution, speedily become a part thereof,—We, the said delegates, in the name and in the behalf of the people of the state of Rhode Island and Providence Plantations, do, by these presents, assent to and ratify the said Constitution. In full confidence, nevertheless, that, until the amendments hereafter proposed and undermentioned shall be agreed to and ratified, pursuant to the aforesaid fifth article, the militia of this state will not be continued in service out of this state, for a longer term than six weeks, without the consent of the legislature thereof; that the Congress will not make or alter any regulation in this state respecting the times, places, and manner, of holding elections for senators or representatives, unless the legislature of this state shall neglect or refuse to make laws or regulations for the purpose, or, from any circumstance, be incapable of making the same; and that, in those cases, such power will only be exercised until the legislature of this state shall make provision in the premises; that the Congress will not lay direct taxes within this state, but when the moneys arising from impost, tonnage, and excise, shall be insufficient for the public exigencies, nor until the Congress shall have first made a requisition upon this state to assess, levy, and pay, the amount of such requisition made agreeable to the census fixed in the said Constitution, in such way and manner as the legislature of this state shall judge best; and that Congress will not lay any capitation or poll tax.

Done in Convention, at Newport, in the county of Newport, in the state of Rhode Island and Providence Plantations, the twenty-ninth day of May, in the year of our Lord one thousand seven hundred and ninety, and in the fourteenth year of the independence of the United States of America.

By order of the Convention.

DANIEL OWEN, President.

Attest. Daniel Updike, Secretary.

And the Convention do, in the name and behalf of the people of the state of Rhode Island and Providence Plantations, enjoin it upon the senators and representative or representatives, which may be elected to represent this state in Congress, to exert all their influence, and use all reasonable means, to obtain a ratification of the following amendments to the said Constitution, in the manner prescribed therein; and in all laws to be passed by the Congress in the mean time, to conform to the spirit of the said amendments, as far as the Constitution will admit. Amendments.

I. The United States shall guaranty to each state its sovereignty, freedom, and independence, and every power, jurisdiction, and right, which is not by this Constitution expressly delegated to the United States.

II. That Congress shall not alter, modify, or interfere in, the times, places, or manner, of holding elections for senators and representatives, or either of them, except when the legislature of any state shall neglect, refuse, or be disabled, by invasion or rebellion, to prescribe the same, or in case when the provision made by the state is so imperfect as that no consequent election is had, and then only until the legislature of such state shall make provision in the premises.

III. It is declared by the Convention, that the judicial power of the United States, in cases in which a state may be a party, does not extend to criminal prosecutions, or to authorize any suit by any person against a state; but, to remove all doubts or controversies respecting the same, that it be especially expressed, as a part of the Constitution of the United States, that Congress shall not, directly or indirectly, either by themselves or through the judiciary, interfere with any one of the states, in the redemption of paper money already emitted, and now in circulation, or in liquidating and discharging the public securities of any one state; that each and every state shall have the exclusive right of making such laws and regulations for the before-mentioned purpose as they shall think proper.

IV. That no amendments to the Constitution of the United States, hereafter to be made, pursuant to the fifth article, shall take effect, or become a part of the Constitution of the United States, after the year one thousand seven hundred and ninety-three, without the consent of eleven of the states heretofore united under the Confederation.

V. That the judicial powers of the United States shall extend to no possible case where the cause of action shall have originated before the ratification of this Constitution, except in disputes between states about their territory, disputes between persons claiming lands under grants of different states, and debts due to the United States.

VI. That no person shall be compelled to do military duty otherwise than by voluntary enlistment, except in cases of general invasion; any thing in the second paragraph of the sixth article of the Constitution, or any law made under the Constitution, to the contrary notwithstanding.

VII. That no capitation or poll tax shall ever be laid by Congress.

VIII. In cases of direct taxes, Congress shall first make requisitions on the several states to assess, levy, and pay, their respective proportions of such requisitions, in such way and manner as the legislatures of the several states shall judge best; and in case any state shall neglect or refuse to pay its proportion, pursuant to such requisition, then Congress may assess and levy such state's proportion, together with interest, at the rate of six per cent. per annum, from the time prescribed in such requisition.

IX. That Congress shall lay no direct taxes without the consent of the legislatures of three fourths of the states in the Union.

X. That the Journal of the proceedings of the Senate and House of Representatives shall be published as soon as conveniently may be, at least once in every year; except such parts thereof relating to treaties, alliances, or military operations, as in their judgment require secrecy.

XI. That regular statements of the receipts and expenditures of all public moneys shall be published at least once a year.

XII. As standing armies, in time of peace, are dangerous to liberty, and ought not to be kept up, except in cases of necessity, and as, at all times, the military should be under strict subordination to the civil power, that, therefore, no standing army or regular troops shall be raised or kept up in time of peace.

XIII. That no moneys be borrowed, on the credit of the United States, without the assent of two thirds of the senators and representatives present in each house.

XIV. That the Congress shall not declare war without the concurrence of two thirds of the senators and representatives present in each house.

XV. That the words "without the consent of Congress," in the seventh clause in the ninth section of the first article of the Constitution, be expunged.

XVI. That no judge of the Supreme Court of the United States shall hold any other office under the United States, or any of them; nor shall any officer appointed by Congress, or by the President and Senate of the United States, be permitted to hold any office under the appointment of any of the states.

XVII. As a traffic tending to establish or continue the slavery of any part of the human species is disgraceful to the cause of liberty and humanity, that Congress shall, as soon as may be, promote and establish such laws and regulations as may effectually prevent the importation of slaves of every description into the United States.

XVIII. That the state legislatures have power to recall, when they think it expedient, their federal senators, and to send others in their stead.

XIX. That Congress have power to establish a uniform rule of inhabitancy or settlement of the poor of the different states throughout the United States.

XX. That Congress erect no company with exclusive advantages of commerce.

XXI. That when two members shall move and call for the ayes and nays on any question, they shall be entered on the Journals of the houses respectively.

Done in Convention, at Newport, in the county of Newport, in the state of Rhode Island and Providence Plantations, the twenty-ninth day of May, in the year of our Lord one thousand seven hundred and ninety, and the 14th year of the independence of the United States of America.